MESSAGE TO THE READER:

To everyone who read this book. I hope that you found a part in here that you could relate to and, if you have any addictions of any kind, I want you to know that my prayers go out to you as you read this, that you may overcome all of them.

Give Glory to God, let him fight the spiritual battles that you can't. Don't ever be afraid to chase all of your dreams, they will come true if you have faith in yourself.

Keep God first, stay strong and never give up until you die. Remember, "A winner never quits, and a quitter never wins!" Live your life to the fullest; cherish every moment of it. Life is too short, so live every day as if it were your last. Thanks for your support and may God bless all of you!

Sincerely yours,
James La Ray Soil, A.K.A. "$miley"

BU
NO

Warning: Graphic material inside.

This book is based on a true story. Some of the names have been changed to safeguard the identity of the characters portrayed.

Dedications

This book is dedicated to my grandmother, Rosie Parker-Yerger (RIP), my mother, June Marie Soil (RIP), my father, James Lee Soil (RIP), Aunt Louise Yerger (RIP), Uncle Sonny Yerger (RIP), Uncle Leroy Yerger (RIP), Uncle David Yerger, my cousin, Debra Boyed (RIP) and my dear friend, Tony "World" Freeman (RIP). All of them played a vital role in my life, and helped create, shape, mold and construct me into the person that I am today. I love and miss you all!

Acknowledgements

I would like to thank every person that I ever came into contact with while living on this earth. Whether it was good or bad, positive or negative, your influence made me want to succeed and helped me to become a better person.

I appreciate all of my teachers and football coaches from Head Start to College. I remember all of you and it seems like it was only yesterday when you were giving me knowledge and instructions.

To all of my family and friends who stuck by me through my successes and failures, you were always there when I needed a shoulder to cry on, or someone to talk to. You never allowed me to give up, even though I had let you down at times. I love you for that.

I would like to say a special thanks to my sister, Tonnetta Laird-Hampton, for always being there for me, from the beginning to the end, and never turning your back on me. Our mother brought us up like that and I know she's looking down on us, proud that we stuck together through thick and thin because that's how she raised us.

I want to thank all of my uncles, Sonny Yerger (RIP), John Yerger, David Yerger (RIP) and Leroy Yerger

(RIP). All of you influenced me and I can honestly say that I have some of each and every one of your traits inside of me. I want to thank my son, J.D. Soil and my daughters, Kawanda Soil and Jasmine Rice-Soil. You all are my inspiration and the light of my life. I also would like to thank Yanina Merritt, who came into my life when I was at my lowest point and stood by me through all of my ups and downs, for never giving up on me. Also, the kids—Katie, Norman and Kimberly.

I want to thank all of my friends and homeboys from Venice, Santa Monica, and Culver City. We had some great times growing up, I wouldn't trade those experiences and moments for anything in the world!

I want to thank my brother Aaron and sisters Sophia and Tricy Soil, I love all of you.

Last, but not least, I want to thank all of my cousins. There are too many of you to name, but you know who you are. Thank you for all the memories that we shared on every Fourth of July, Memorial and Labor days, those barbecues were the best.

I want to give a shout out to all of my dead homies, all of my homeboys from Venice Shore-Line Crips, my homies from Santa Monica, Culver City, and the homies that are locked up in the penitentiaries throughout the state of California. Keep your head up, cuz, we eagerly await your return home.

A special shout out to author Shane Lorde, who inspired me to write this book after reading his book, Why Good Men Go Bad. and my investors, Donald Brown and J.O. Entertainment. Thank you, guys, for helping me complete this book.

Cover designed by: Wahida Clark Publishing

Special thanks to my assistant technical adviser: Norman Merritt

Contents

CHAPTER 1

Back in the Day

I remember how it all began. I was nine years old living in Santa Monica, California. I had seen and been around drugs from an early age because my mother, her sister, and all of my uncles were drug abusers, as were my father and his four brothers. Back then they got high on prescription pills, not the opioid pills of today, but Barbiturates, with street names such as Tuinals, Red Devils, Black Mollies, Yellow Jackets, Codeine, Quaaludes, and Valiums—just to name a few. The sad part about it was that these were all prescription drugs provided by a licensed physician by the name of Dr. Shannon Bum.

I will never forget that name because he was the one who started it all.

My mother's name was June. She was the most gorgeous and loving woman I had ever laid eyes on. Her smile could light up a room and she often went out of her way to help other people. She worked as a seamstress; her and my Aunt Louise could sew clothes exceptionally well. They would buy patterns and raw materials from the fashion district in downtown Los Angeles and make clothes for themselves, my sister, and my cousins.

After work, my mother would always bring my sister and me little cheap toys home to play with such as those wooden airplanes, Jacks, and coloring books. It didn't matter what it was, we always appreciated whatever she brought us.

To me, my mom was the best mother in the world. Although she wasn't perfect, I loved her dearly. She and my father divorced when I was two years old. After their split, my father came around from time-to-time, but not as much as I wanted him too. My father's name was James; he was a tall, handsome man, at least six feet, four inches who worked for the City of Santa Monica as a trash truck driver.

I remember one day I was waiting for his truck to come down our block. I knew it was coming because of the loud noise the truck made from picking up those big, green, metal trash containers, flipping them above the truck, releasing the trash, then slamming the huge trash bin back to the ground. It sounded like thunder to my little ears.

I stood there waiting for him as the truck made its way down my street. He got out of the truck and I ran and jumped into his muscular arms. He picked me up saying, "Hey son, how are you doing?" I replied, "Ok, daddy!" with a big smile on my face because I was happy to see him. I felt so tall when he held me.

He asked, "Are you doing good in school?" and "how's your mother?" I said, "Yes, I'm doing good in school and mommy's fine!" He then reached into his pocket, gave me a white envelope filled with money and said, "Take this home to your mother." I hugged him really tight, told him that I loved him, jumped down, and took off running home. I did not stop for anything until I reached my front door out of breath!

I gave my mother the envelope while saying proudly, "I just saw daddy and he told me to give this to you!" She took the money, smiled, and said, "It's one thing about your dad, he was always good to me." My mother loved my dad, that's why she said she kept his last name. Although my father and I never played catch with a baseball or football, I loved and respected him regardless.

After my mother and father divorced, she met another guy named Sonny and they had my little sister

Tonnetta. That relationship did not work out and all the ones that followed would turn out to be worse.

It was the early 70's and life for me as a kid was at its best. My friends and I played outside all day, something that kids today don't do. It seemed as though we never ran out of things to do and explore. There were always enough of us kids, so if we wanted to play football, baseball, or basketball we would have enough players to make up two teams.

When we got tired of playing sports we played games like hide and seek or tag, and if we got bored with that, we found construction sites and took the old scrap wood to make go-karts. We rode them down a long hill on 20th street that we called "20th Street Hill." It was our little own racing strip. Riding those go-karts down 20th Street Hill was so much fun; the wind would be blowing in our faces as we raced the wooden carts down the hill at full speed.

One of the most fun things we did was to go beneath our apartment complex; the complex was very large and U -shaped.

We put on old baggy clothes that we found in garages at the back of the apartments, so we wouldn't get the clothes we already had on dirty, and crawled under the complex with flashlights.

It was a great big maze down there. We pretended to be secret spies while crawling on all fours as we made our way around the complex, stopping below certain apartments to hear other people's conversations above us.

We started at one end of the complex and came out on the other side. It would be pitch dark down there, even with the flashlights. We could only see what was in front of us, nothing at the sides, I guess that was what made it scary and fun at the same time.

As night fell and the street lights came on my mom would call out my name. That's when I knew it was time to come in, "La-Ray, La- Ray! It's time to come in!"she would say. I raced home because I knew it was time to eat.

My mother was a great cook; it would be one of many things that she would teach me to help me survive later on in life. When I came into the house she would have the table set and say, "Go wash your hands, boy, and come sit down and eat!" I said, "Ok, momma!" and did just what she said because I would be starving from running around playing all day.

We lived in a one-bedroom apartment with a den. My sister and I shared the den with bunk beds and my mom had the room, of course. Tonnetta was two years younger than me so I would have to look out for her. We used to watch the old "Batman and Robin" together all the time. The two of us sat right in front of the television and sang the song when the show came on. "Batman, Batman, Batman!" At the part when Batman and Robin would shake hands, we turned to each other and shook our hands at the same time. I was Batman and she was Robin.

I also played Pop Warner football. My mother signed me up because she felt that it would be good for me to play, but she also believed it would toughen me up.

Some of my other friend's mothers had signed them up as well; we all ended up on the same team, the Santa Monica Vikings. I liked playing football, but I had never played contact football with real equipment before, so when we started hitting I didn't like it that much anymore.

One day after practice, I made up my mind that I was going to quit—or so I thought. I went home and told my mother that I didn't want to play football anymore and, being a mama's boy, I thought she was going to say, "Ok, baby, you don't have to play." When I arrived home she was in the kitchen preparing dinner. I walked in and my mom said, "Hi La-Ray, how was your day? I know you're hungry from football practice." I said, "It was okay!" with a voice that suggested something was wrong.

My mother said, "What's the matter? They worked you too hard today?" I took a deep breath and replied, "Momma, I don't want to play football anymore!" I will never forget what she said to me after that. She quickly turned from the stove, bent down to where our eyes met, and said, in a stern and serious voice, "Boy you are not quitting football and you're going to practice tomorrow. Now get out of my face before I whip your ass!"

I turned, put my head down and wanted to cry, but I knew that if I did, I would have gotten my ass whipped right there on the spot. So, I just headed to my room while saying to myself, "My mother doesn't love me anymore, she's trying to get me killed out there." Little did I know, by making me play and not letting me quit, she would soon change my life forever.

I ended up playing football after all and it wasn't as bad as I thought. Besides, we played every day in our apartment complex and that gave me an edge. I was placed at running back because I was fast and quick, and I scored one or two touchdowns every game. I think the reason why I scored so much is that I was running for my life because I didn't want to get hit. My mom only came to one of my games; she always said, "I'll come to your next game when you go pro!" Now that I look back, I wish she would have come to more, after all, she signed me up and I really could have used her support.

When the season was over, we had a banquet, but I couldn't make it because we didn't have a ride.

One sunny afternoon I was outside playing and I saw this familiar looking white guy pull up in a car. After he parked and got out, I realized it was my football coach, Mr. Williams. He started walking towards me with a smile on his face and something shiny in his hand. When he got closer I saw it was a trophy. He handed it to me and said, "You did a good job, James. We hope to see you next year!" He shook my hand, turned and walked back to his car.

I immediately ran inside the house to show my mother the trophy I had just received. She was sitting at her sewing machine making clothes when I busted in the door yelling, "Momma, Momma!" She turned around and said, "Boy, what's wrong with you making all that noise?" I said, "Look momma, I got a trophy for playing football. My coach just brought it to me!"

Her face changed into the big beautiful smile that I always loved to see and she said, "Awe my baby got a trophy, come give me a hug, I'm so proud of you La-Ray!" I gave her a super big hug and watched her as she smiled, admiring the first of many trophies that I would give to her. There was nothing I would love to do more than to make my mother smile and be proud of me. I continued to play football throughout my youth, dreaming—as all young boys do at that age—that one day I would go to the pros, buy her a spacious house and truly make her proud of me.

Those were the good old days. As kids we didn't have a care in the world, our mothers made sure we had all that we needed and, most of all, they gave us unconditional love.

My grandmother, who was an exceptionally sweet lady, lived next door to us. I truly believe we got our upbringing from her. She was also a pure and spiritual lady I swear it seemed as if she and my great aunts went to church every other day. They all met at her apartment—Aunt Mary, Big Momma, Aunt Geneva, and Aunt Jenny. All of them wore fur coats, funny looking hats and a lot of costume jewelry. I will never forget the smell of that old lady perfume that would linger in her living room after they left to go to church. She made us kids go to church on Sunday too, and when she wasn't at church or bible study,

Grandmomma was always busy doing something. She had so much energy for an old lady. Granny would be cooking, cleaning, washing clothes and singing church songs, all at the same time.

I loved my grandma, she was the most willful person that I have ever been around. All of the kids met at her house for breakfast in the morning because our mothers were working then. She had eggs, bacon, toast and orange juice waiting for us when we came over. We ate breakfast and headed off to school and Grandma always said, "I don't want to hear any unpleasant reports at school today, y'all hear me?" We answered, "Yes Ma'am!" at the same time. We had to say"Yes ma'am" or "No ma'am," we couldn't just say yes or no to her. We had a different type of respect for Grandma. Don't get me wrong, we loved our mothers dearly, but Grandma was like God.

We couldn't get away with anything when she was around. She watched us like a Hawk, we couldn't even whistle around her. One time my cousin and I were just learning how to whistle. We were sitting on her back porch whistling away when her voice came out of nowhere and said, "Alright y'all better stop that whistling out there!" We didn't think anything of it at first; we just looked at each other in confusion like she has to be kidding and started whistling again.

Then she said, "Alright, I done told y'all about that whistling. I'm going to go out there, get me a switch and spank your butts—out there being mannish!" We just laughed in silence, it was crazy, but little did we know she was teaching us how to be respectful. My grandmother was real old school, she grew up in Hope, Arkansas, and moved to California later when my mother and her siblings were teenagers. She was a good, old-fashioned country girl and we loved her dearly.

My mother's older sister, Louise, and her three kids, Debra, Kevin, and Reynard, lived in the same apartment complex. My Aunt Louise didn't take any shit; she was more streetwise and hip to the game than my mother at the time. The real shady characters came over to her apartment because she could do hair real good. Back then it was processes, perms and finger waves. There would be nothing but gangsters, hustlers, dope dealers and players over at her apartment waiting to get their hair done and making drug deals.

My cousins and I sat around watching and listening to these guys talk shit until our moms made us leave. My Aunt Louise would say, "Y'all know better to be sitting around in grown folks' faces, now get your little asses out of here!" We would scamper into the bedroom, still peeking out to watch the show that was going on in the living room. They would be jammin' to the legendary sounds of Al Green, The Isley Brothers, Four Tops, Marvin Gaye, Stevie Wonder and all the other old school musicians.

We were amazed by the guys' outfits with crazy colors, butterfly collars, platform shoes and tight bell bottom pants. We never knew their real names, but they all had nicknames, like Weepy, he was a tall, humongous, black ass nigga, a real mean looking dude. I don't know why they called him Weepy because he didn't look like the type of guy who cried.

Then there was a guy called Bull, who was also a tremendous sized nigga. He was the enforcer and his head was extraordinarily large, just like a bull's head.

Then there was a guy called Stack of Dollars, aka the Moneyman. He was real slick-looking and kept wads of cash in his pockets.

Last, but not least, there was a guy called Black Gold and he was black as oil, so I guess that's why they called him "Black Gold." I believe he was the main dealer because every time someone had to talk to him they would go into the next room, close the door and lock it. I always thought that was strange.

All of these guys sat around drinking and smoking cigarettes that had a funny smell to them. They also had white powdery stuff that they would crush up on the coffee table and sniff up their noses. Keep in mind, we still didn't know what drugs were, but we knew something wasn't right. We were curious about the white stuff they kept putting up their noses and those cigarettes with the funny smell.

My Aunt Louise would have one guy bent over the kitchen sink washing the treatment out of his hair, my mom would be putting those giant pink Styrofoam rollers in another guy's hair, and there would be one more nigga under the hair dryer. It was as if they had their own gangster beauty shop going on.

They played the same songs over and over all day; my Aunt Louise loved Al Green. Whenever the song "Let's get married today" came on, she screamed and said, "Oh that's my song!" Like I said earlier, we never ran out of things to do, from running around playing outside with our friends, to watching the shady characters that would come to my aunt's apartment to get all flied up.

13

It didn't stop there. I also had four uncles who were all into the same game. As a matter of fact, they were all good friends and partners with the guys who came over to my aunt's apartment. My Uncle Sonny was the eldest. He was tall and slim with a gigantic ass Afro. He was the funny one of the bunch always laughing and joking. He kept a Colt 45 malt liquor in his hand.

My Uncle John. He was real chilled and laid back, but if you made him mad it would be over and he would kill you.

My uncle Dave was just as crazy, but in an offhand way.

I remember one night he was so high on prescription pills that he was standing in front of the mirror trying on my Aunt Louise's wigs. My cousin and I watched in amazement as he put on one wig and started posing like a person would do when trying on a hat. He took off the wig then put the other one on; my cousin and I looked at each other then looked back at him and just laughed in silence. He never knew we were watching him. Little did we know we were witnessing the side effects of drugs and how they could change a person's personality because my uncle wasn't gay.

Uncle Leroy was the player of the crew. He would pull up in his light blue Cadillac convertible dressed real sharp from head to toe. He had a pretty woman wrapped around his arm at all times.; I always wanted to be like him.

They called my uncles The Yerger Boys! That was their last name and if you fucked with one, you had to fuck with all of them!

CHAPTER 2

Welcome to the Hood

Although I had seen drugs, and the people who came over to my aunt's house to use and purchase them, I didn't know what they actually were for or their purpose.

I will never forget that day. It was early evening and my friends and me were walking home from football practice. As we got closer to the apartment complex we could see a lot of police cars. As we entered the apartment complex, one of my neighbors frantically ran up to us and said, "The police just kicked in your aunt's door and took your mother, Louise and everyone else that was in there to jail for drugs!"

I was confused and dumbfounded because I didn't know what drugs actually were, but I began to put it all together. The cigarettes with the funny smell, the pills and the white stuff they were putting up their nose were all drugs. The guys that came over to my aunt's apartment were drug dealers. They were drug users too, which included my mother and aunt.

Hours later they got bailed out of jail and when they came home, it seemed as if everything had changed at that very moment. My mom was crying; she said to my sister and me, "Baby, I'm sorry, mommy didn't mean to get into trouble!" She hugged us and we all cried together.

We were evicted from our apartment. We moved to Los Angeles for a short time then to a place called The Jungles in Baldwin Hills, and finally to Venice, California, where all hell broke loose.

Although we lived ten minutes from the beach, the Oakwood area we moved to was a one-by-one-mile community where all the poor blacks and Latinos lived. It was an extremely active area where drugs and gang activity prevailed.

Growing up in Venice, my cousins and I had to meet a whole new group of friends and these guys were not playing hide-and-seek or pushing go-karts, they were hardcore gang members called the Venice Shoreline Crips! They called themselves that because they were the last gang on the Westside and the shoreline of the Pacific Ocean ended there. We had to learn a whole new way of life and how to survive because those days in Santa Monica were long gone.

When I was about 14, I began to notice that the prescription pills had begun to take more control of my mother and auntie. Even though it was gradual, I could see a change in them for the worse; something just wasn't right. They did everything together, you wouldn't see one without the other, so when they moved into the house in Venice, it became a horrifying drug haven. Before the crack epidemic, it was prescription pills that they would get from their doctor to sell to other people.

It was years later that I would learn how they got so many pills. One day, my cousin and I were reminiscing about those dreadful days. He said to me, "Remember when we used to go to the doctor with our moms and we would have to sit in the car for hours?" I said, "Yeah, they would be there forever it seemed." He then said, "They were in there having sex with Dr. Shannon Bum to get all those pills." My heart just dropped. He was older at the time, so he knew what was up; he just didn't want to tell us then because we were too young to understand.

I first saw my mother intoxicated on prescription pills when I came home from school one day. I went inside the house and saw her at the dinner table, her face was lying in a plate of food that she had been eating. I thought she was dead so I ran over to her, shook her and said, "Momma what's wrong?" She spoke with a sluggish sound that I couldn't understand, but she was saying my name, "Laa-Raaay, Laa-Raaay."

I will never forget the sound of her voice from that day, and whenever I hear it like that afterwards, I knew she was high off of the prescription pills. I cleaned the food from around her face and helped her to her feet. She couldn't walk, so we staggered to her room. I cried and sat there with her because I didn't know what was wrong. I put a cold towel on her face and all she could do was mumble my name.

As time went on, my mother's addiction got worse and the company she and my aunt kept got worse as well. The house we moved into became a place for heroin addicts, pill poppers and small time petty hustlers. It got so bad that when we woke up in the morning, there would be different people in our house from partying the previous night, some even took it upon themselves to move in, suitcases and all.

My cousin and I said fuck it and moved into the back garage we called it the Back House! It was all freaked out with aluminum foil we stole from the local supermarket, which we then wrapped around the walls and the ceiling. We hung up those fluorescent posters that glowed in the dark, and you know we had the infamous black light. For music, we had an old 8-track stereo that we stole from a car. We stole car batteries every other day to power it and listen to jamming songs by Parliament Funkadelics, Earth Wind & Fire, Cameo, The Ohio Players, Barry White and all the other old school funk jams that were out back then.

About that time, all supervision had vanished and we pretty much did what we wanted to do. My mother and aunt did their thing in the front of the house and we did ours in the back. I don't know whether they didn't care or if it was just the drugs because it seemed as though we all were living separate lives and the prescription drugs were tearing the sheer fabric of our entire family apart.

When we got bored, we would sneak around to the front of the house, and peek through the broken glass windows, to see addicts shooting up heroin in their arms, people popping pills, having sex, counting money and selling drugs. Yes, our mothers were right there in the mix; it was very sickening, disgusting and disturbing to watch, but we did anyway.

We were little perverts too. When our mothers' female friends would pass out in one of the rooms, my cousin and I would sneak in there and have sex with them. Here we were, 14 and 16 years old, having sex with grown ass women who were doped out of their fucking minds. Or were they? For some strange reason they kept coming back for more. I guess you could say we were some pathetic little motherfuckers because we were friends with some of the kids of the ladies who would pass out. Little did we know, watching and participating in these strange activities would slowly be inherited into us as teenagers.

As parental supervision lessened, my cousin and I grew closer to the boys in the hood and became a part of The Venice Shoreline Crips, they were now our new family.

One time my cousin Debra was badly beaten and raped by this guy named Big Joe. I believe he tried to kill her, but she survived, however she would never be the same again. One day me and my Crip homeboy named Bub were chilling in the Back House listening to some music. All of a sudden he turned down the music and said, "Word on the street is that Big Joe did that to Deb!" Bub was like family, so he wouldn't lie about something like that, he even lived with us from time to time. He had this look on his face like nigga now that you know, what are you going to do about it? Her brother was nowhere around, so I had to go handle it by myself.

Big Joe lived down the block from us. I took off walking down the street to confront him about the situation. As I was walking down the street, I could see him standing in front of his house. My heart started pumping extremely fast and I could feel the adrenaline running through my body.

I walked up to him and asked, "Why did you do that to my cousin?" He had this little smirk on his face and said, "Lil nigga, you better get the fuck out of my face before I fuck your ass up too!" He was bigger than me, but a sloppy, fat, obese big, not muscular. I knew I could take him because I was quick and good with my hands.

I stole one punch to his nose and blood immediately started to gush out everywhere. I jumped on him, grabbed him in a headlock, and used his body weight to flip him onto the ground. I got on top of him and I just started beating the shit out of him as if I were a mad man. (It's one thing about me, I'm a real chill guy, but if you do something to me or my family I'm going to try and kill you).

I could hear people yelling and screaming, "Don't break it up, that nigga raped his cousin!" That made me fight even harder. I was getting the best of him, so they finally pulled us apart, but not before I made him apologize. I said, "Say you sorry nigga, say you sorry!" He said, "I'm sorry man!" as he wiped the blood from his mouth. He respected my family and me from that day on; that would be one of many fights I would have in Venice to gain my respect!

Although I wasn't into drugs yet, it was soon to come. My cousin and I began to get more involved in the gang lifestyle. We would roam the streets of Venice at night with our new family, the Crips. With no more home supervision at all, and no care in the world, we felt invincible, getting wilder and wilder as each day went by. We started robbing people, stealing cars, committing home burglaries, snatching purses, fighting and anything else we could do for the thrill of it. Our innocence as little kids was long gone, a fragment of our imagination.

We were Shoreline Crips now and there was no turning back. We had a new meaning in life. Anything we could steal we would take it and we stole something every day. I got my nickname Smiley from doing "licks." Licks are when a person goes around robbing and stealing to make money. I would come back around my homeboys after I did a lick and would be smiling. One day, my homeboy got hipped to me and said, "You just did a lick, huh? I can tell when you do a lick because you always come back smiling, I'm going to start calling you Smiley!" After that, everybody started calling me Smiley.

As time went on we terrorized our community. A white person got robbed right there on the spot; if they were a wetback, we would wait, catch them coming from out of the bar drunk, then rob and beat them; If they were a Mexican, it was straight out war. We stayed fighting with the Mexicans in the other Venice gang called the V-13's. It seemed as if every summer we would go to war with each other over turf just to see who would run the hood.

I remember one time an all-out racial war broke out, the blacks against the Mexicans. That summer alone, over 50 people were shot and 22 were killed. At that time, if a person wasn't "Gang Banging" they had better not have been on the streets of Venice after dark. It had gotten so terrible that the police didn't even come down there after a certain time. The only reason the killing stopped was because mothers and children started getting killed; both sides called a truce and the killing would stop for now, but the war still continues until this day!

My first year at Venice High was immensely different for me because the campus was exceptionally large and I wasn't prepared for it. I still had that street mentality; not knowing I was at a place that was preparing me for my future. It didn't dawn on me until I went to the football game one Friday night and heard the band playing and seen all the people in the stands, and some of the guys I knew out there on the field getting ready to play. They weren't into drugs or gangs. Right then I said to myself, "I'm playing football next year no matter what, but for now it was all about Crippin."

I started selling marijuana when I was in the tenth grade; I was still a hustler and a Crip. It kind of bothered me that I missed my freshman year of football to gang banging and running the streets of Venice. Prior to that, I had never missed a year of playing, but the hood was trying to take me under.

At lunchtime, I would sell the white kids parsley rolled up into joints. It started off as a joke at first, but they kept coming back for more. I couldn't believe it; I said to myself, "They're actually buying this shit, dumb asses!" I would make money from scheming the white kids, then buy real weed to sell to the niggas because they weren't going to fall for that parsley bullshit.

One day after school I was in the Back House rolling up my joints to sell at school the next day while listening to some Parliament Funkadelics, which was my favorite group back then and still is to this day. The song I was playing was called "P-Funk" and the chorus went, "Make my funk the p-funk, I want to get funked up. I want the bomb, the p-funk, don't want my funk stepped on!"

My homeboy Bub walked in and said, "Man, why are you always listening to that shit and you ain't never been fucked up before?" I looked up at him and said, "Fuck it, cuz, let's go get fucked up!" We left the Back House and started walking to Oakwood, that's the name of the park where all the homeboy's hung out at. We were looking for one of our older homeboys to buy us something to drink because we were too young to buy it for ourselves.

We got to the park, but couldn't find anybody old enough just then my homeboy Billy Clark pulled up. He was the same age as us but, back then, that nigga was as husky as a mother-fucker and he looked like a grown ass man. We asked him to take us to the liquor store to buy some "Crip juice." Crip juice is some cheap ass wine called Silver Satin that we used to mix with Kool-Aid because it tasted nasty as fuck. Then we would shake it up real good and we had our "Crip juice!"

He said, "What ya'll niggas know about some "Crip juice?" Then he said, "C'mon get in, I'm going to get ya'll niggas fucked up." We said, "Hell yeah, let's go!" We jumped into the car and headed to the corner liquor store. Billy was a wild dude, he reminded me more of a country ass nigga then a nigga from the hood, he was always loud. He kept saying, "I'm going show ya'll niggas how to get fucked up!"

We pulled up beside the store, gave him some money and he went into the store, but when he came out, he had a large bag filled with bottles, way more than we had given him money for. I mean, Boone's Farm, Silver Satin, Mad Dog 20-20, Bacardi, Ripple, Old English and some other cheap ass liquor.

We said, "Damn! Cuz, you didn't have to get all that shit." He said, "Y'all said you wanted something to drink, so let's get fucked up, cuz!" and he just laughed, "Ha-Ha!" He had this crazy, loud ass laugh.

I'm not going to lie, I began to have second thoughts after seeing all that alcohol, but it was to late, the peer pressure was on. Billy jumped in the car and we took off. We went driving all over Los Angeles drinking, smoking and tripping. We smoked about four to six joints, mixed all those drinks, we wanted to get fucked up, and that's we did.

After driving around for a while, getting wasted, my head started to spin. I could feel myself getting ready to throw up so I rolled down the window and threw up all over the side of the car and everywhere else. Never before in my life had I felt so sick. My homeboy Bub was fucked up as well; Billy just laughed as we were laid out in the back seat, tossing and turning. He took us to the Back House, dropped us off and said, "I told y'all I was gonna get you fucked up!"

He jumped back into the car, still laughing, and I could hear him say as he was leaving, "Ha-Ha ya'll niggas, ain't ready!" as the car sped off burning rubber. The next day, after I had sobered up, I realized that I had smoked and drank too much because I didn't know my limit, but after that I knew how much I could handle. I stayed high every day to escape all of the bullshit that was going on in the front house and the downfall of my mother and aunt.

Marijuana and alcohol would be my gateway for other drugs that were soon to come in a vicious cycle, I was becoming like my mother getting more and more addicted to drugs and alcohol. Studies have shown that drugs and alcoholism can be inherited through family members. I believed that this was happening to me; we were becoming a dysfunctional family being taken over by drugs.

One day, when I was walking home from school, I saw smoke coming from afar. I didn't think anything of it, so I stopped and talked to some of the homeboys before I headed home. The sirens from the fire trucks became louder, and as I got closer, I could see the fire trucks passing me and stopping at my house. I started running to see what was going on. When I got to the house, I could see that someone had burned our Back House down, all of my clothes and stuff were inside there, I had lost everything. I remember the fireman coming up to me, handing me a black 8 ball and saying, "This was the only thing left!" It was weird because I had never seen that 8 ball before.

By then, things were spinning more and more out of control. My mom and aunt were on those prescription pills really bad and were not paying rent, or any of the other bills. It had gotten so bad and embarrassing that my mom would be passed out on the street. My homeboys would come find me and say, "Cuz, your mom is passed on the curb on 5th Ave, you better go and get her!" That truly tore me up inside and made me realize that I would never see that beautiful side of my mother again, she was now a fully-fledged drug addict, hooked on prescription pills. I went over to the block and could see people trying to help her up. I just ran over, grabbed her and carried her home with tears running from my eyes.

I used to wish, hope, dream and pray that one day my mom would get off those prescription pills, and that we would be a real family again, but that was just a dream. She was gone and our lives would never be the same. I was so hurt, and I felt cheated; the prescription drugs provided by a licensed doctor had taken the purest person that I loved the most in this whole wide world.

About a week later, I was on my way home from Oakwood Park. When I got there I saw my mom, aunt, sister and cousins standing in front of the house, with all our belongings wrapped in sheets lying on the sidewalk with the Sheriff there. We had been evicted. I was ashamed, but more so, I felt so sorry for my aunt and mother because they had hit rock bottom. Years before this they were two beautiful Black Queens with a healthy family, jobs and full of life, joy and happiness; now this.

We moved into another apartment building around the corner and this spot was just as horrendous because the building was owned by one of the biggest heroin dealers in Venice. They called him S.D. my Aunt Louise used to be one of his girlfriend's so he let us move into the apartment on the proviso that they sold drugs for him and let him use the apartment for a stash house.

Although my Aunt Louise and my mother didn't inject heroin, prescription pills had a hold of them. It seemed like they didn't care about their appearance anymore and they just let themselves go. One morning I woke up hearing my cousin Debra screaming out to my mom, "Auntie, come check on my mother, she's not breathing!" I immediately jumped up and ran into my aunt's room to touch her hand to see if she were warm. I used to do this to my mom when she was asleep to make sure that she was okay, because I never knew when that time would come.

I touched my Aunt Louise's hand and it was cold as ice, I knew she was dead. I turned her over and could see the imprints from the bed spread on her face. I have never forgotten that look to this day.

My Aunt Louise was gone; she died from an overdose of prescription pills provided by her family

31

doctor. I loved my auntie, she laughed a lot, made clothes, styled hair and she was a fantastic cook.

Her death took a toll on the whole family. My mother was devastated because, not only did she lose her sister, but her best friend as well and, as any loving sister would do, she took in my three cousins, after all, we were always together.

My cousin Kevin was in Youth Authority at the time which was a jail for minors. The death of his mother took a toll on him as well because when he got out of jail, he said, "fuck it" and seriously started gang banging full-time. That's how he got his nickname Crazy Crip Kev!

He started smoking Sherman, PCP and Angel Dust which is all the same thing, just different methods of doing it. He just didn't give a fuck anymore and went back to jail for robbery, burglary and some other bullshit. His mom and my mother were family and best friends. Kevin and I were the same way, if you saw him you can best believe that I was somewhere close by. When he went back to jail, I lost my cousin and my best friend as well. I knew how my mother felt because we were like our mothers, two peas in a pod.

Luckily, I played football when I was younger so I realized I had better play this coming year or I would be doomed. Football was my passion and I hoped it would be a way for me to escape the harsh reality of the life I was living, seeing my cousin and all my other homeboys going to prison and getting killed. I figured I had better get back into it or I would be next!

My sophomore year in high school came, I tried out for football, and played on the B team. Although I was playing football, I was still in the hood fucking up, committing petty crimes, and my mother's appetite for prescription pills didn't go away either. Things would get worse   and   worse   as   time   went   by.

CHAPTER 3

(Free Base) The Epidemic

Upon my graduation from high school, I didn't have any future plans. I had hoped of an athletic scholarship to play football, but that was just a dream. My varsity year was not very impressive and we finished the season on a losing note. I was nowhere near ready for college any damn way.

By that time, a new drug came out and, not only did it sweep my community, but also every black community across the nation as well. It was called Free-Base Cocaine, it was supposed to be hip and chic, all the so-called trendy rich people did it. The actor Richard Pryor tried to burn himself up while getting high on it; an up-and-coming basketball star, named Len Bias blew his heart out, after signing a lucrative professional contract. He died from consuming too much of it.

The drug made a folk hero out of a local drug dealer named Freeway Ricky Ross! I'm talking about the Real Rick Ross and not the fat ass, fake rapper who used to be a prison guard Ricky Ross, he was the first major drug dealer in Los Angeles dealing with the Colombians, until he got caught up in that Ronald Reagan, Oliver North and Contras Affair bullshit, but that's another story.

I will never forget the first day I saw Free-base in action; some of my older homeboys were doing it at one of their houses. I was with one of my friends named Tony Freeman, on the streets we called him World because he knew everything about the world, or so it seemed. World and I were just hanging out at our older homeboy's house when one of them pulled out a plate with coke on it, a glass pipe, some Bacardi 151, and some Ether. I had never seen it done that way before, but I remembered when my uncles and their crew were doing it, they put it up their noses, they didn't smoke it.

I just sat there watching them doing some stuff as if they were mad scientists. Lighting up a cotton swab attached to a piece of wire, twirling a little glass bottle around then pouring the liquid from it onto a plate and letting it evaporate. I said to World, "What the hell is this shit, cuz?" He replied, "You will see, just wait!"

Then one of the big homies pulled out a razor blade and started scraping it around the plate. We could see the cocaine start to pile up; I swear it looked like some kind of magic trick or something. I just sat there watching out of curiosity. He then put some of the powder from the plate onto a glass pipe, dipped the cotton swab into the 151 Bacardi, set fire to it, put the fire to the pipe and began inhaling real slow. I could see the thick white clouds of smoke fill the glass pipe.

As he inhaled, and blew out the smoke, his eyes got strangely wide, he couldn't talk for about five seconds. After that, the rest of the big homies went into a frenzy to see who was going to hit it next.

After they all had taken a hit of the pipe, they were sweating, and breathing fast and hard. I was like damn! Look at these motherfuckers, they're tripping. We stayed and watched in amazement. Then one of the big homies asked if I wanted to try it and, like a fool, I said, "Yeah!" trying to be down, but little did I know I was headed for self-destruction. He put the pipe to my lips, lit it and said, "You gotta hit it slow."

I hit it, but I thought it was like weed, so I inhaled kind of fast and blew the smoke out. He said, "Damn! Cuz, you hit too hard, you're wasting it." My mouth got real numb but, other than that, I didn't feel anything unusual—I guess I did waste it.

World then said, "Let me show you how to hit, Smiley, you don't know what you are doing, cuz!" The big homie put some more coke on the pipe for World and lit it; I could see the white smoke going through the pipe. He held it in and then blew it out, his eyes got real wide, he started licking his lips real fast and said, "That's how you hit it, cuz!" I could see he was breathing hard as well.

We hung out over there for a while longer, watching them argue over the next hit. They kept wanting more and more until they finally ran out of coke and didn't have money to get more.

Then one of my big homies named Adrian said, "Let me get $20 from you, Smiley." I said, "Here cuz," and gave it to him. I didn't have a choice, he was my big homie so I had too. I gave him the money and then World and I left; I was surprised that he asked me for $20, Adrian was one of the guys in the hood who always had cash on him.

It would be about a month later when I would have my second encounter with cocaine. This time it would be much more different because I was at World's mother's house and he had the coke this time. He said, "I'm going to show you another way how to do it, Smiley!"

We went into the kitchen where he had a pot of water boiling on the stove, a small bottle and some baking soda. He poured the powder cocaine into the smaller shaker bottle along with a little water and some baking soda. I always watched in confusion because these guys never finished high school, yet they were doing something that you would think they learned in a chemistry class or something.

He put the smaller bottle in the boiling water and started twirling it around. The next thing I saw was the cocaine in the smaller bottle beginning to bubble and gel up. He pulled the little bottle out of the boiling water, added some more baking soda and began to twirl it again, this time in cold water. After a while, I heard something clicking in the bottle. He said, "You hear that?" I said, "Yeah!" He emptied out the rock cocaine on a paper towel and said, "That's a rock!"

He then pulls out a glass pipe, similar to the one the big homies had, cut off a piece of the rock with a razor blade, put it on the pipe, then pulled out a lighter and said, "You gotta hit it really slow, like this, Smiley." He put the fire to the pipe.

While he was hitting it, I could see the white cloud of smoke moving slowly through the glass, he blew out the smoke and his eyes got really wide, it looked as if he were in a trance or something. He said, "Damn! Cuz, that was a good one. Are you ready for yours?" Like a dummy I said, "Yeah!" He got the pipe ready for me, lit it up and said, "Hit it real slow, Smiley." I did just what he said.

I could see the white cloud forming into the pipe as I inhaled the smoke into my lungs. I blew out the smoke, I must have hit it the right way this time because I felt this tingling sensation go from the top of my head to the bottom of my feet, it felt as if I just had an orgasm or something. Now I know why their eyes were getting wider—because cocaine made a person paranoid.

I said, "Damn! Cuz, that shit is good give me another one!" I didn't know it at that time, but I had just inhaled the Devil into my soul, and he would haunt me for what seemed like forever. World took another hit and passed it to me, I was like a veteran now—I knew how to hit it!

We smoked for about four hours, it seemed as if time had just flown by. After a while we ran out of coke and World wanted to get some more. I said, "Man, I'm high enough, I don't want anymore. I'm cool cuz!" Cocaine is one of those drugs that you can't get enough of, the more a person does, the more they want. Since I was still in my early stage it hadn't gotten to that point yet, but little did I know it was soon to come.

World had started smoking before me and I think it was starting to get a hold on him. He would say to me, "Smiley, this shit seems keeps calling me cuz!" I said, "Let's just chill and we can get some more later." He replied, "No! Cuz, just give me $20 and I will give it back to you tomorrow."

He had this strange look in his eyes that I had never seen before— a look of desperation that could kill. World was my homeboy, and I knew if I didn't give him some money, he would go and get it somewhere else, by any means necessary, so I gave him $20 and said, "I'm out!" Then I left.

It was a late night, or should I say early morning, about 4:30am, as I walked down the dark streets of Venice heading to my girlfriend's house. I was paranoid, and it felt as if something or someone was watching and following me. All of a sudden, I saw two headlights from a car slowly coming down the block behind me.

As the car crept closer and closer I started to walk faster, because at the time you never knew when those Mexicans would catch a nigga slipping and bust a cap in your ass. When the car got closer I realized that it was a truck. As it passed me, two guys in the back jumped up with something in their hand and, in a panic, I took off running, thinking that the Mexicans were going to shoot me.

They then threw something over my head and it landed in the front yard of a house. It was the damn newspaper truck with the guys in the back throwing the morning paper to the houses! I was high and tripping; my mind was playing tricks on me.

As I got closer to my girlfriend's house I could feel little cravings. I wanted to go back to World's house for more, but my girl was expecting me, and I was already late. My girlfriend was a lovely, clean cut square girl named Kim. I met her at Oakwood; park she was 18-years-old at that time and a cashier at the neighborhood grocery market. She and her sister shared an apartment on 6th and Broadway.

She was an innocent, skinny, and sweet girl. When we first met, earlier, before we hooked up, I would always tell her how pretty she would look if she let her hair down. She kept it in a bun and would say, "I will one day," and she would just smile at me. She had the prettiest smile.

I was a street dude. I seriously didn't think that she would talk to a guy like me.

41

One day I walked into the store to get some Zig Zag rolling papers and some chips, and as I made my way to the check out stand, I saw this tall cashier with long, black, silky hair down to her shoulders. I thought to myself, they must have hired a new girl. As I got closer I could see that it was Kim. I put my stuff on the counter; she looked up with a smirk on her face and said, "You should stop smoking weed so much!"

I tried to change the subject by complimenting her on her hair. I said, "Damn, girl, your hair looks nice, I didn't even recognize you. I told you that you would look good with it down!" "Thank you, but you still should stop getting high so much!" I replied, "I will if you let me have your phone number, so I can get high off of you instead." She smiled, "I'm going to hold you to that," and gave me her number. We were together ever since then, but I never stopped smoking weed.

When I arrived at her apartment, I knocked on the door and Kim opened it with her T-shirt and panties on.— She always had this innocence about her, but she was a freak in bed. We went into her bedroom, I was still coming down from my high, Kim didn't know what I had just finished doing, but she knew something was up.

I took off my clothes, got into the bed and laid next to her. She said, "Why is your heart beating so fast and why are you sweating so much?" I just told her about the truck and that paperboy situation—not that I had been smoking cocaine with World. After I had told her how scared I was, she just laughed and said, "I bet you will get your ass here earlier next time!" In my mind, I was thinking about World and wondering if he bought more coke.

My mind was saying, "Yes I want more," but my body was saying "no." Kim held me tight, as if she knew what I was thinking. As our bodies got closer, I could feel my dick rising. We started tongue kissing and I was getting extremely horny. I put my hands between her legs and her pussy was soaking wet. I pulled her panties down and got on top of her. She grabbed my dick and slid it into her pussy—it was wet, warm, and tight. She wrapped her long legs around my back, let out a loud moan and said, "Oh yes, baby, I've been waiting on this dick all day. Oh, oh! Give it to me baby, give it to me, fuck your pussy, good baby!"

She always astonished me when we made love because she was so shy, but when we would fuck I would see a different side of her. We fucked all that night. I don't

43

know if it were the Coke or what, but I couldn't stop fucking her.

When we finally took a break, we were both dripping with sweat. She looked me in the eyes and began crying. I started laughing at first because I thought she was playing, but she was not. I said, "Baby what's wrong?" She said, "Ray don't ever leave me!" I stopped laughing and said, "Awe baby, you know I would never leave you, I love you!" She replied, "I love you too, that's why I said don't ever leave me!" I said, "I won't, I promise you!" We kissed and held each other; the craving for the coke went away and we fell asleep in each other's arms.

I dibbled and dabbled with cocaine for a while. It was now the early 80's and we didn't have a clue what damage and destruction this drug called "Freebase" was about to do to the people in black and latino communities throughout America. As time went by, freebase cocaine was on the rise. A lot of my homeboys were getting deeply involved into drugs, killing, getting killed and going off to prison.

Selling freebase cocaine was the new way to make a lot of fast and easy money. At that time, if a person wasn't selling cocaine, they were smoking it. As time went on, some of my homeboys were transformed from gangsters to drug dealers and drug abusers by this new drug epidemic that was sweeping the nation. I said to myself, "You're next. All of your boys are going to prison or getting hooked on cocaine, you're going to be next." I had to figure out a way to escape this madness, what could I do, where would I go? How could I get far, far away from this place that used to be called home, but was now a death trap?

I had to use my street smarts and get myself out of this situation one way or another, so one day I decided to go to one of those military recruitment offices to see what my options were to join the service. This could be a way for me to escape for sure, I could get far away from the hood as possible. There was no other choice, but death or prison, and it wasn't going to be either of the two.

The next day I went to the recruiter's office, they had posters of all of the branches of the service, along with different brochures. I was immediately greeted by one of the recruiters, he said, "Hello young man, how are you doing today?" I said, "Fine sir!" trying to be respectful. He was dressed in the traditional Navy uniform like the guy on the Cracker Jack box. "So you're thinking about a career in the military, huh?" "I was thinking about it sir," I replied.

He told me his name was Petty Officer Richards, and that if I had any questions feel free to ask him. He then asked, "Is there any particular branch you were looking into?" I said, "the Navy or Air Force maybe," I knew it wasn't going to be the Army or Marines because I wasn't going to be rolling around in the dirt and doing all that shit I had seen on the commercials. I wanted an adventure.

He gave me his card and some brochures to take home and said, "The Navy would be a good experience. You could learn a skill, make some good money and travel around the world." At that time, that's exactly what I wanted to do; travel as far as I could to get away from the negative environment that I was now in. Don't get me wrong, I loved my hood to the end, but I knew that I had to leave or I would be just another statistic lost to the ghetto streets. Besides, with all the death and destruction that was going on in Venice, somebody had to make it out and I made up my mind that I would try to be one of them!

I thanked him, told him that I would think about it, and took the brochures that he had given me home to read through them. I liked what I saw and decided right then that I was going to enlist in the Navy. I told my mother the good news. She said, "That would be good for you." She was still in her drug induced world, so I didn't think it mattered to her one way or another what I did at that time. Kim was happy for me as well as some of my homeboys.

I went back a week later to see Petty Officer Richards and informed him that I had made up my mind to join the Navy. He said, "You made a good decision recruit Soil, now let me get you all set up!" I took all the required exams and passed all the tests. After signing my life away, I was now enlisted in the United States Navy.

They put me in the DEP program, and I would be sworn in within the next two months. DEP stood for Delayed Entry Program, it allowed a person to spend time with their family before reporting to boot camp. I was like, "Fuck it, I'll be gone in two months I might as well get high on coke as much as I can before I leave." It was actually just an excuse for me to get high. Back then a person was called a Closet Smoker! That was before the term crack head! came out. You didn't see the effect of cocaine on people like you do today, with the loss of weight, missing teeth and homelessness.

Two months went by; I had partied like a rock star. Now my orders had come, it was time for me to report to boot camp. I hoped that I would leave the drugs and street life behind me and not end up dead, in prison or hooked on drugs. I had believed by going to the Navy that it would save me, but it was too late. I had already been exposed to a world I could never escape from, the world of free base cocaine I had smoked it and now the genie was out of the bottle and couldn't be put back in!

Two more months went by. I had completed boot camp and received my orders to report to my ship, "The USS FFG Walls," which stood for United States Ship Fast Frigate Walls. It was stationed in San Diego, California. That was my first mistake because I was only two hours away from home. My second mistake was that the ship was brand new, so it stayed docked for a year to undergo tests before it was to be deployed. This allowed me to go home on the weekends with money and that's when my troubles continued.

My mother had moved to the Mar Vista Gardens, The projects in Culver City, California, while I was in boot camp. It's funny how they name the projects like they're some luxurious estates or something. The projects were just another hellhole, I don't care what they named them, we were still in the ghetto. By then they stopped calling it "free-base cocaine or rock cocaine," Crack was the new name. The epidemic was in full effect, I mean everyone was either on it, or had somebody in their family who were. Either way, it had begun to destroy people, their families, and black and latino neighborhoods throughout the country.

I remember coming home from leave one day and I just had this urge inside me to get high, I don't know why, especially after being clean for several months. I didn't know how to cook cocaine then, but I remember watching my homeboy World cook it. I'm the type of person that if I see a person do something once, I can mimic them and do it. I'm a quick learner and sometimes that's not good.

My cousin had got out of jail and I wanted to celebrate, another excuse to get high. So I said to him, "Cuz, I got to show you this new shit niggas are doing to get high!"

I bought an eight ball of coke; we went to a head shop on Venice beach, bought a glass pipe and a small shaker bottle, and then went back to my mother's house.

I will never forget that day, it would be the day that I would introduce crack cocaine to my entire family, just how my homeboy World, had introduced it to me, including my mother.

As I sit and write this book, it brings back a lot of unpleasant memories, things deep down inside of me that I would like to forget about. To this day it still hurts, I regret what I have done, but I must tell my story in hopes that people young, old, African American, Latina, Asian, Caucasian or whatever your nationality is, that you will learn from my pain, suffering, and sorrow, and not get involved with drugs of any kind.

CHAPTER 4

In the Navy

The next couple of pages were extremely difficult for me to write because I did something that would change my family's lives forever. I got a pot, filled it with water, put it on the stove and the water began to boil. Everybody was watching me, Kevin, my sister and her friend Lisa, I could tell by the look on all their faces they were dumbfounded, as I had been when I had first seen it.

I put the coke and some baking soda into the shaker bottle and then put the bottle in the boiling water. As it started to gel, I held it under the cold water and started twirling it. When the gel hardened and started hitting the side of the bottle, I said, "You hear that?" They said, "Yes!" I replied, "That's a rock!" Then I poured it out onto a paper towel.

I then pulled out the glass pipe, put a piece of crack on it, lit up my torch, and took a hit. They were all looking at me with a look of astonishment and curiosity at the same time. My eyes got really wide, I started breathing rapidly as I prepared the next hit; mind you, this was the first time that they had ever seen this kind of shit, so they didn't know what to expect.

I asked my cousin, "Are you ready to try this shit cuz?" I pushed the pipe toward his lips. "You got to suck it in real slow or you're gonna fuck it up!" He hit just like I told him and blew out the smoke, it looked as if he had an outer body experience, he just laid back in the chair and said, "Damn! What is that shit? It got my heart beating fast like a mother-fucker, I can't feel my mouth." I replied, "I told you this shit was a trip!" I prepared a hit for my sister.

I told her how to hit it, she did what I said, and then I pushed the pipe to her lips. She took a hit, blew out the smoke, and immediately went to sit on the couch and started to rock back and forth. I said, "Are you alright?" She shook her head, yes, her eyes were large as silver dollars, she was high as fuck.

I fixed her friend Lisa a hit and said, "Are you ready?" She nodded yes and leaned forward to take her hit. I lit the pipe and told her to suck it in slowly, she did just that. When she blew out the smoke, her eyes began to dilate, she stood up and looked at me as if I were the devil, which I probably was at that time then she ran out of the house!

After Lisa ran out of the house and slammed the door behind her, my mother came down the stairs and said, "What are y'all doing down here?" I tried to hide the pipe and coke, but she knew something was up because everyone was quiet and acting strangely. At that time it didn't matter because we pretty much did what we wanted. Then she said, "I know what y'all doing, y'all down here smoking that stuff!" The next thing she said shocked me and broke my heart at the same time.

"Let me try some of that stuff, boy?" I told her, "No, mom, you can't do this, it's not for you!" She replied, "Boy! I've been getting high before all of ya'll." I should have just left the house right then and there, but I didn't.

I loved and respected my mother dearly, although she was abusing prescription drugs, and was not the person I knew as a little boy. Now I was about to do the unthinkable, introduce her to crack cocaine and get high with her as well.

I know people are reading this and shaking their heads and saying, "What a scumbag, how could he do such a thing?"

I said to her again, "Mom you can't do this!" She was so far gone on the prescription pills that I couldn't reason with her. She asked again, but in a more serious tone, "Let me have some, hell you're doing it in my house!" I regretfully fixed her a hit, at the same time shaking my head in disappointment and disbelief.

I put some coke on the pipe and told her what to do. She took a hit, blew out the smoke, started breathing hard, sat on the couch and said, "I want another one!"

We smoked for the rest of the night with the money I had brought home from leave. I didn't have a clue what I had just done to my family because the crack epidemic was so new, we didn't know what the hell we were messing around with.I had just introduced my family to one of the worst drugs in the world. How could this be? Considering how much I hated drugs when I was younger.

I was now becoming a mirror image of my ancestors, continuing the curse of drug abuse. I would have never imagined this happening in my lifetime, it had to be some kind of conspiracy because it happened fast and it affected so many people and their families. We didn't have those shows like Intervention back then, if we had, we would have been the perfect family for it.

As time went on, my motivation grew more for drugs and less for the Navy. I started breaking into lockers on the ship to support my ever-growing drug habit, I was not myself anymore, I was now losing control.

One day. I was on the ship and had received a call from my mother. I thought that was strange because she had never called me while I was on the ship before.

I picked up the phone and my mother was on the other end crying uncontrollably. I said, "Momma what's wrong?" She replied, "Granny's gone!" I said, "What do you mean Granny is gone?" Deep down inside I knew what she meant, I just didn't want to believe what she said. I broke down and started to cry. I told her, "I have to put in a request to leave the ship so I can come home." I hung up the phone, went to my bunk, closed my curtains and cried all night.

At that time I had so much going on, losing motivation for the Navy, my battle with cocaine and the death of one of the most influential people in my life. I was living a lie and my life was a mess. I never put in an emergency request for leave and I didn't attend my grandmother's funeral. I just wanted to remember her for how she was loving, caring, sweet and strong-willed woman. I miss her to this day.

After the death of my grandmother, I began to question myself and the lifestyle that I was living; I fell into a deep depression. After all, I was supposed to be the one who made it out of the hood, the one to break the family curse and become someone, but it was the opposite. Instead, I was doing drugs, ruining my life, my relationship with Kim, my career in the Navy, and letting my family and friends down. I would hold on, but only for a while.

My ship finally received orders to deploy for a series of tests in the Pacific Ocean, afterwards we would set sail to Hawaii. I was relieved because this is what I joined the U.S. Navy for. The commercial that got me was the one that said, "The United States Navy... it's not just a job, it's an adventure." I was ready for my adventure, ready to get as far away from the projects, and drugs as I possibly could. This would be my first deployment and my first time traveling across the country, especially on a ship.

It took us two weeks to sail to Hawaii. When we finally arrived it was one of the most exotic places that I had ever seen in my life, clear waters, blue skies and beautiful people. The strange thing about it was that after we arrived in Hawaii, I had never once thought about cocaine, it seemed as if it were all behind me. I was in

Utopia! I never wanted to return, I was excited and happy to be in a different environment, all I could think about was that I was in Hawaii, far, far away from the projects.

We set anchor there for two more weeks, every day my fellow shipmates and I just enjoyed the island, going shopping, Luau's, clubs and sightseeing. Reality set in when it was time to sail back to the naval base in San Diego, I was on my way back to hell.

I desperately wanted to stay there in Hawaii or just sail around in the ocean doing more tests, anything but go back to the world I had just left.

My rank was E2, it stood for Enlisted Engineman, and my duty was to make fresh water out of seawater, and to provide the ship throughout with air-conditioning and refrigeration. One night, on the way back from Hawaii, I was on duty patrol making my rounds in the engine room on the bottom of the ship, checking all the pressure gauges and temperatures, making sure that all systems were going.

All of a sudden, I heard something banging up top, so I walked up the stairs to see what it was. When I got up top, I headed towards where the sound was coming from, it led me to the berthing area where the lockers were. When I got there, I saw the locker door swinging back and forth as the ship rolled from the waves. My first intentions were to close the locker, instead I looked inside, and saw a white envelope. I pulled the envelope out to see what was inside, it was nothing but 100-dollar bills, 15 of them to be exact.

The first thing I thought about was how much coke I could buy when I returned home. It was as if a demon had taken over my mere thoughts, only if that locked wouldn't been opened, I would have continued doing my rounds on the ship.

The temptation was to strong and I was to weak. I took the envelope, stuffed it down my pants, closed the locker and put the lock back on it as if it were never opened. At that moment it seemed as if this evil spirit was inside of me and guiding my every move, I had no control over it. Although I had been in the navy for almost a year, I still had that street ghetto mentality that wouldn't go away, here I am on watch, and I'm the one that they should have been watching.

Immediately after I was relieved from my dutyI quickly went to my bunk, closed my curtain, pulled out three envelopes and pretended to be writing something. I put the money into the envelopes, along with some paper to make them look like letters, dropped them into the mailbox on the ship and mailed them home to my girl Kim.

The next day the Captain of the ship got on the loudspeaker and reported that $1,500 from a locker was missing from aboard the ship. The MP's would be doing a full search of everyone's locker and personal space. Little did they know the helicopter had come earlier that morning to pick up all the mail; that money was long gone off the ship and on the way to my girlfriend's house.

I had no self-control; the drugs had taken over me. I had been exposed to and had done so much evil at a young age that I couldn't stop hustling even in the Navy. There is an old saying that, "You can take a nigga out of the ghetto, but you can't take the ghetto out of the nigga!" At that time, I guess you could say I was living proof of that.

I called Kim a couple of days later to see if she had gotten the money I had sent her, she said yes and asked, "Where did you get it from?" I said, "I just been saving it up; go buy yourself something nice and put the rest up until I come home."

A few weeks later when the ship arrived back in San Diego, I took a taxi to the bus terminal and caught the bus home. It was strange how I could be away and not think about drugs, but when the opportunity had come to steal, as it did on the ship that night, just like that I would be ready to get high and be back in that same negative environment where the demons were, and they were waiting for me.

I arrived at Kim's house. Usually we would make love immediately upon my return, but this time I just hugged, kissed her and asked, "Where is the money?" She went into the bedroom brought it out to me and I was on my way out the door.

She asked, "Where are you going? I want you to fuck me, I've been waiting a month for you baby." I said, "I have to go take care of some business, I'll be right back!" She then said, "I know where you're going, you're going to smoke that stuff, people have been telling me that you're on it and now I see. Please don't go, Ray!" She hugged me, so I wouldn't leave, I pulled away from her as if the drugs were calling me. I left the house as she cried and begged me not to go. My mind was already made up, I ignored her cries, went to find my cousin and my homeboy Bub, so we could get high with the money I had stolen from the ship.

I found them at Bub's girlfriend's house. They were already smoking and were about to run out of coke, so they were extremely happy to see me because they knew when I came home I always had some money and this time I had a lot.

I knocked on the door, Bub said, "Who is it?" I replied, "It's me, Smiley, open up the door." He opened the door, "What's up, cuz?" We shook hands, my cousin was sitting at the table with the pipe in his hand and said, "What's up, Smiley? 'Bout time your ass came home, come hit this nigga!" He handed me the pipe, I took a big hit and sat my ass down because it had been a while since I had smoked.

I then pulled out a pocket full of money and said, "Let's go get some more. I did a lick on the ship and came up." They said, "Damn! Nigga you did come up, let's go, we were almost out!" We jumped in Bub's car and went to go see the dope man.

We smoked all that night and the rest of the next day. I had never smoked that much coke and for that long before. The drug was taking more and more control over me; I could feel Kim slipping away. I went to Kim's house, after my 24-hour drug binge, looking a mess and all burnt out.

I knocked on her door and she opened with a disgusted look on her face and said,

"You've been smoking that stuff, look at you, you can't even talk right!" I was just rumbling out of my mouth, trying to make up lies about where I had been, but she knew because I had taught her well, she was not a dummy. She then said, "I told you that stuff is not good for you and if you keep on doing it, you're going to lose me Ray!" She was getting older, prettier, and the other guys were starting to take interest in her.

She started seeing a change in me and how drugs were quickly beginning to have an effect on me, robbing me of my very soul. Kim was what we called a "square, a good girl" and I was a "unruly street dude." It seemed as if the Navy couldn't change that. As time went on the double life I was living was starting to catch up with me, I was serving in the U.S. Navy and doing crack cocaine when I would come home. How could I keep this up? I couldn't, soon it would have to all come out into the open.

My ship deployed again, we would go out to sea for another month conducting tests, playing war games, that was my only escape from drugs and the projects. When the ship returned to port, I went straight over to Kim's house. I didn't tell her that I was coming, I caught the first greyhound bus to Los Angeles, then the local bus to Kim's apartment. In my heart I could feel something was going on, but I didn't know exactly what.

When I arrived at her apartment, I just walked in without knocking. To my surprise, when I walked in, there was this nigga sitting on the couch. My instincts were right, I knew this nigga from back in the days, his name was Marty Hill. I said, "What's up cuz?" with a mean ass look on my face. His eyes got bigger than a motherfucker, like he had just seen a monster, he was caught by surprise and had no idea that I would be coming over there that day.

I proceeded to walk to Kim's bedroom to ask what the hell this nigga was doing over at her apartment. She was in the bathroom, doing her hair as if she was going somewhere. She was surprised to see me as well, she played it off, hugged, and kissed me as if there were nothing going on and said, "Hey baby, I didn't know you were coming home today, why didn't you call me and let me know?"

I replied, "I was going to surprise you, why is that nigga Mark over here?" Kim said, "Oh he just came over to talk baby, he knows that I'm with you!" Either she was lying or playing it off real cool, or both. I said, "Well, it's time for him to leave before I kick his ass!" I proceeded back into the living room to tell him to go, but to my dismay he was already gone. I then walked back into the bedroom and asked, "Are you fucking him or what?" She answered, "No Ray!" I replied by saying, "You're a damn liar, why is he over here then?"

I'm not the kind of guy that gets off on hitting women, but no bitch or nigga is going to play me. I grabbed her by the neck and said, "Who have you been fucking then, while I've been gone?" She said, "Stop choking me, you're hurting me!" Then she just blurted out, "It wasn't him, it was somebody else!"

I was shocked, heartbroken, and confused at the same time. How could she do this to me? After all, I thought I had her under control, but then I knew from my drug use it was just a matter of time before I would lose her. I asked, "Who is it then?" She said a name that would just throw me off, "Steven, it was Steven!"

I couldn't believe it, Steven was one of those square ass niggas from the hood that didn't gang bang, do drugs or any of the street shit that I was into, we even played high school football together. I slapped the shit out of her and her nose started bleeding, then I left her house to find Steven, so I could beat his ass too.

As I was leaving Kim fell to the ground and was holding on to my leg, crying and begging me not to go because she knew I had a temper and that maybe I would kill him or something. She cried and said, "Please don't go Ray, I'm sorry, I didn't mean to hurt you!" and all that other bullshit, but I was hurt and mad, there was nothing she could say or do to stop me.

She said, "Things are not the same anymore, you're always gone, and when you do come home you go off with your boys to smoke cocaine. It's taking more and more control over you and I just got lonely." I looked at her in disgust because I truly loved her, I would have never imagined in my mind that she would do such a thing. I pulled my leg away from her, grabbed her car keys off the table and was out the door before she could grab me again. All I could hear was her crying and begging me not to leave saying, "Please don't go over to his house, it wasn't his fault!"

I jumped in the car, started the engine and was burning rubber as I sped off heading down the block to that nigga Steven's apartment. I knew just where he lived, in my homeboy World's apartment complex on the second floor. I pulled up to the complex, got out of the car and started yelling for him to come down. "STEVEN, STEVEN, YOU UP THERE!"

I kept on yelling his name when he finally came to the window and said, "Soil, what's up man? When did you get back in town?" I replied, "I just came home today, come down, I need to talk to you about something." Steven said, "Alright, I'm on my way." He didn't know that I was about to split his head open for fucking my girl while I was gone.

He came downstairs smiling and as he reached his hand out to shake mine, I immediately punched him in the face with a combination of one right fist to the nose and a left hook to the eye. Blood started running from his nose as he backed up and tried to cover his face. He yelled, "Soil man, what's up? Why are you tripping?"

I hit him again, this time in the jaw, as he tried to run around the side of the car for cover. I said, "You done messed up by fucking my girl while I was gone out to sea!" He put his hands up, while continuing to back up around the car, then he said, "No man, let me explain it wasn't like that."

"Well how was it then, nigga?" Still standing in my fighting position. "He said, "Please man! You gotta let me explain it to you, she came onto me." Shocked, I said,

"What the fuck are you talking about?" Steven replied, "Don't hit me anymore, I can explain everything!"

I put my guard down and let him talk as he wiped the blood from his nose with his t-shirt. He knew I had a reputation in Venice and that I could get real crazy, so I let him tell his side of the story.

I said, "Nigga! What happened? I want to know everything or I'm going to fuck your ass up some more." He started to explain saying, "Man, I swear, one night we were hanging out at Friday's in the Marina Del Rey, me, her friend Kay-Kay and my boy Shawn, having a couple of drinks just chilling. When it was time to go they wanted to stop by the store. We went inside the store, me and Shawn were getting something to drink and they were over in the magazine section laughing. Then Kim called me over; her and Kay-Kay were looking at a Playgirl Magazine. Out of the blue Kim asked me whether I was I bigger than this guy or that guy in the Magazine.

I knew she was tripping because they were drunk and besides, you guys were still together. I just played it off and said, "Girl yall trippin let's go."I went to pay for my stuff and got back into the car. When they got back in Kim said, "You can drop off Kay-Kay first and then Shawn.' As soon as I dropped my boy Shawn off she was all over me. I pushed her away and said again, "Girl you're tripping, I'm taking your drunk ass home." She kept on kissing and rubbing all over me, I'm sorry man there was nothing I could do, she wouldn't stop!"

We were still standing in the street talking when people started gathering around and looking out of their windows to see if we were going to fight some more.

Steven said, "I swear to God I didn't come on to her man, it was almost as if she forced me to, I don't know if it was the alcohol or what!"

I looked him directly in the eyes and I knew he was telling the truth. Kim was right, I had been gone and when I came home, I was doing drugs. She always said that I would lose her if I kept on doing drugs, I guess she wasn't lying. I had to give Steven a pass that day, no man is going to turn down some pussy, unless he's gay. I said, "My fault man, don't trip." I shook his hand, got back into the car, feeling like a complete idiot, and went back to Kim's house.

When I arrived back at Kim's apartment she was laying on the couch still crying with a towel on her nose. I told her that Steven had told me everything that happened and then I asked, "How could you do me like this? I thought you loved me?"

"I love you baby, but like I said, you're gone all of the time and when you do come home we never spend time together anymore like we used too. You're always with Bub and Kevin getting high, I just got lonely. I'm sorry baby, I didn't mean to hurt you, please, please forgive me!" Kim's plea went unnoticed as I said, "You broke my heart, you were my first love, you let me down, and now I can't trust you, it's over. I don't want to see you anymore!" I turned and walked out of the apartment.

She ran after me crying, pleading, and trying to hug me. I just pulled away from her and left. My plan was to use reverse psychology and make her continue to beg for me back, after all, I thought had taught her everything she had ever known. What I actually did was create a monster because before we started going out, guys weren't interested in her, now she had gotten hot headed as more and more guys started noticing her. My plan backfired, she never begged me back. Shortly after we broke up she started dating a basketball player from some college and eventually ended up getting pregnant by a fireman.

I had lost my first love. Deep down inside I knew it was the drugs. With all of the rumors going around, after losing Kim, I spiraled further into a depression and my addiction to crack got even worse.

69

One night, after a weekend binge on drugs, I couldn't take it anymore. I hopped on the greyhound bus still tweaking from the coke. I had all kinds of thoughts running through my mind as I made my way back to the ship.

My mind seemed as if it was racing a million miles per second, it felt as if it were about to explode. I had reached a place that many people know as rock bottom. I asked myself, "How am I going to pull myself out of this one?" I had to think fast and pray to God to deliver me from this wickedness.

I was always a survivor from the streets and when my back was against the wall, it made me fight that much harder. I would have to make a serious decision because I was in the fight for my future and my for my life. Right then I said to myself, "Fuck it! I'm done with this coke shit." I began to hate it as much as I use to love it, I decided that when I got back to my ship I would tell the chief doctor about my drug problem and seek help for my addiction.

CHAPTER 5

Daddy's Gone

I arrived at the ship late that night. The long bus ride brought me down from my high and depression would set in. Back to reality, back to acting like my life was intact, when in fact, to say the least, it was a complete mess. I reported to the officer on duty, then went to my quarters, and laid down on my bunk thinking about my past and how my life has changed since I started abusing drugs. The vicious cycle of becoming like my parents, losing Kim and living a double life because no one on the ship had the slightest idea that I had a problem with drugs.

I never brought drugs onto the ship, I was always on time to my workstation and performed all my duties with no problems. I had left the streets of Venice to be something, but now it seemed that I was in a worse position than before. I had to get out of this one. I would have to expose my situation to the doctor the first thing in the morning. Totally drained, I closed my eyes and went to sleep.

The morning came and I reported to my station as usual. After count I went to my first class petty officer for a request to see the ship's doctor. My petty officer asked, "Is everything alright Soil?" I replied, "Yes, I'm just feeling kind of light headed." I was not about to reveal to him what my real problem was that I was coming off a coke binge, and that I was hooked on drugs. He wrote me out a chit to go see the doctor.

As I made my way to his office I began to have mixed emotions and wondered what was going to happen to me once I revealed my situation. My performance on the ship was good, I had never gotten into any trouble, but I was scared that I would get kicked out because of my drug use.

I had no choice because I was headed for self-destruction and I needed help. I went down to the infirmary, gave the nurse my chit, told him my name, rank and that I was here to see the doctor. He took down all of my information and said, "Take a seat Mr. Soil, the doctor will see you in a moment." I replied, "Thank you!" and took a seat.

After a few minutes the doctor came and said, "Hi James, what's going on? You feeling okay?" It was a small ship, so everyone pretty much knew one another. I didn't know how to tell him because he reminded me of one of my old football coaches when I was a young boy, I didn't want to disappoint him.

I paused for a second with tears running down my cheeks. He asked, "What's wrong James? Are you still grieving over your grandmother?" I shook my head no. "What's the problem then?" he asked again with a more concerned voice. He came and sat beside me as I wiped the tears from my eyes. I looked at him and said, "I think I have a drug problem!" He then replied, "What are you talking about James, You're one of the best enginemen we have on the ship. What kind of drug problem?"

I kept looking at him and said, "I've been smoking crack cocaine and I think it's starting to affect me, I need some help sir!" He looked at me with a confused look on his face and replied, "Smoking crack cocaine! What is that and why James?" Back then, crack cocaine was a street drug and upper-class white people didn't have a clue about it, they were more into snorting. I explained to him that it started off as just an experiment and I just started doing more and more. The doctor then said, "I need you to write down and explain in full detail how you are smoking cocaine because I have never heard of this method before."

He gave me a yellow notepad, and I began writing down how the process is done. I finished the letter and gave it to him; he put on his glasses and began to read it. As he started reading I could see the shock, frustration and disbelief on his face. After reading the letter he asked, "My God! James, how long has this been going on?" I said, "Off and on for about a year and a half. I started before I enlisted in the Navy." the Navy only tested for marijuana, that's how I was able to get away with it for so long.

He then asked, "Are you making this up so that you can get out of the Navy?" I replied, "No sir, I love the Navy. I don't want to get out, that's why I came to you for help, I don't know what to do." He then said, "I'm going to have to send you to the psychiatrist for a mental evaluation. You have to tell him everything that you just told me, understand James?" I replied, "Yes sir!" He then said, "We're going to get you some help!"

He wrote me out a chit and I went to see the psychiatrist immediately after leaving his office. When I arrived to see the psychiatrist to my dismay he was already there waiting for me. The psychiatrist was a black lieutenant. I guess the doctor was really thrown off on what I had just revealed to him and felt that a black man could relate to my situation better, but that wasn't the case.

The lieutenant believed that I really was making up this story to try to get out of the Navy. He made me stand at attention in front of his desk. As he began to question me, he said, "How are you doing Mr. Soil? According to my reports you have a drug problem, is that correct?" "Yes sir, I'm here today seeking help." He then said, "I know you're not trying to get over on me or trying to get out of the Navy?"

I looked at him in amazement because he was black, my superior, and I thought he would be more sensitive to me, as the white doctor was. He continued to ask me a series of questions, as the doctor had done, and I explained to him everything, in full detail, that I had been going through for the past year and a half, as I had explained to the doctor.

I really thought the Navy would help me, especially since I disclosed my problem with drugs rather than getting caught with it in my urine.

After the psychiatrist finished probing with questions about my drug problem, he sent me back to my ship, but not before saying, "Mr. Soil you will need to undergo a mental evaluation to see if you are stable and

healthy enough to serve in the U.S. Navy. You cannot leave your ship until your evaluation is complete, is that understood, Mr. Soil?" I replied, "Yes sir!" and left his office to return to my ship.

On the way back to my ship all kinds of thoughts were racing through my mind like did I do the right thing, are they going to kick me out, are they going to put things together and find out about the lockers that were being broken into? When I arrived at my ship either I was paranoid or my mind was playing tricks on me because it seemed as though all my fellow shipmates were avoiding me, as if they knew something was up. The guys that I thought were my friends would make small talk and move on, giving me the side eye.

I guess the word had gotten out aboard the ship that I was involved with drugs and that all my shipmates should keep away from me. I felt isolated, I had now been exposed, my double life is over now. I was waiting for the Navy to decide my fate and my future.

About that same time my ship was preparing to be deployed on a "Westpac." That's when the ship joins a fleet of other ships and goes across the Pacific Ocean to Japan, the Philippines and other countries across the equator.

They installed a program called Project Upgrade that was designed for all the bad apples aboard ship, to get them out of the Navy before the ships went overseas. By exposing my drug use I qualified for this program that I didn't want to be a part of. I was looking forward to going overseas and seeing all the different cultures and countries, after all, that's why I joined the Navy. That trip would never come to pass. A week later I was called down to the doctor's office. He informed me that I had been added to the project upgrade list, but I would be alright.

I was confused. On one hand he was telling me that I was about to be discharged from the Navy, but on the other hand, he was saying that I would be alright. I said to myself, How can I be alright, if they're going to discharge me from the navy?

A few days later they called all the project upgrade personnel to meet at the administrative office aboard the ship. Me and five other guys where down there.

The doctor came out and informed me, again, that I would be alright and winked at me. I still didn't understand why he kept on saying it, knowing that they were getting ready to discharge me. He came back out of his office, this time with six manila envelopes in his hand, and called out each one of our names.

Each of us opened our envelopes and pulled out the contents that were inside. discharge papers. The first guy said, "Fuck! They gave me a dishonorable discharge." Another guy said, "I got the same thing!" Then the next guy sitting next to me pulled his papers out and said, "I got a general under honorable conditions." He then turned to me and asked, "What did you get?"

I pulled mine out real slow hoping that I didn't get a dishonorable discharge. It said, 'honorable discharge. I was surprised and said, "mine says honorable discharge!" One of the guys then asked the doctor, "Why does he get an honorable discharge and he's getting dismissed like us?" The doctor took my envelope, went back into the office and a few minutes later he returned and handed me back my envelope.

I opened it and it said, honorable under general conditions." The doctor said, "I told you that you were going to be alright, you should have kept your mouth shut!"

He then said, "Gentlemen! You are now discharged from the U.S. Navy, you must leave the ship immediately." We all grabbed all our belongings and the MP's escorted us off the ship.

On my way to the bus station I was mad that I opened my big mouth. I couldn't believe what had just happened, I had just been dismissed from the Navy and I still had a drug problem, what was I going to do now?

When I got inside the bus terminal I found a bench far away from other people and I just cried. What would I tell my family and friends? What was my mother going say? I always wanted to make her proud of me, but for some reason or another it seemed as if I never could. Usually, I would be in a hurry to get home, so I could get high, but this time I wanted the bus to take forever, so I could gather my thoughts. As I boarded the bus, my mind was in a confused state. How was I going to explain this to my mom? After all, she had her own demons to battle.

After the two hour bus ride I finally arrived at my mother's house. I was embarrassed and ashamed to tell her what happened. I opened the front door and my mother

was there sitting at the table talking to her best friend
Carolyn. She was a Christian lady who would come over
to pray and talk with my mother to help her get off drugs.
I walked in and my mother said, "Hey La Ray, what are
you doing home? I thought you were getting ready to go
overseas?" I didn't hesitate to answer her, I said, "I told
them that I had a drug problem and that I needed help,
they dismissed me."

Carolyn and my mother put their arms around me to
comfort me. My mother said, "Awe La Ray I'm so sorry,
don't worry baby, everything is going to be alright."
Carolyn started to pray for me then my mom asked, "What
are you going to do now?" I replied, "I don't know. Can I
stay here until I figure something out?" My mother
replied, "Of course you can stay here, you know I will
always be here for you, baby." I went upstairs to relax,
unwind and contemplate what I was going to do with my
future.

The crack epidemic was now in full effect with gang
violence on the rise and drive-by-shootings occurring all
over the city of Los Angeles for drug territory. Damn near
everybody in the hood was doing coke, even people you
thought wouldn't be on it were now using it. Girls,who in
the past wouldn't give you the time of day, were now on it

and if they didn't have the money to buy it, they would exchange sex for drugs. We called them Strawberries, where that name came from, I don't know, but that's what we called them.

The projects where I lived was one gigantic hellhole, they had a Mexican gang called the Culver City Locos and they ran the projects. It was only one way in and one way out of that place, it was a death trap for other local gangs who would come and try to do drive-by-shootings. Rivals would come in shooting, then would have to turn around, and try to make it back out the same way. They never make it out. I had seen so many murders in that place it was like scenes from a movie. I wouldn't have to go see movies like "Boyz n' The Hood" or "Menace to Society," all I had to do was step outside my front door and all that action would be taking place live, right there in my face!

As time went by I began to adjust to life outside of the Navy. I continued to use more drugs and things got worse because I couldn't escape back to my ship when I ran out of coke, so I would go from crack house to crack house getting high. I couldn't find a job, so I resorted back to my old way of making money, stealing and doing petty crimes to support my ever growing drug habit.

One day I came home from another overnight drug binge to find my mother on the couch crying. I ran over to her and said, "Momma, what's the matter? Why are you crying?" She looked me in my eyes and said, "They found your father dead in some apartments in Los Angeles. He took an overdose of heroin!" I just fell to my knees, distraught, and started crying. Although my father and I didn't have a real close relationship, I loved him dearly. My mom and dad had been divorced since I was two-years-old, but she still loved him as well. She would always tell me that she would never love another man as much as she loved my dad, now daddy was gone.

Drugs had taken another one of my close family members. I was confused and I didn't know what to do. My whole life was falling apart, losing my girl, abusing drugs, getting dismissed from the Navy and now the death of my father, I was distraught. What was I going to do?

Word on the street was that he was in a dope house and went into the bathroom to shoot up some heroin. After about 15 minutes the people he was getting high with didn't hear anything, so they knocked on the door, still no answer. Eventually, they kicked in the door and there he was sitting on the toilet, dead, with the needle still stuck inside his arm. They picked him up and carried him out of the house, then threw him behind some bushes so that the police wouldn't find him in the apartment. I guess you could say he had some good friends.

My depression escalated and I continued doing drugs. What I didn't know at that time was that all the things I was going through then would help shape me and make me the strong-willed person that I am today. Was I depressed? Hell yes, I was depressed, dysfunctional, psychotic, paranoid and everything else that was close to being crazy. At that time, I actually didn't know what depression meant, I thought it was something that old white people went through, not a 20-year-old young nigga from the hood.

One thing I would never do was to blame my parents for how I had turned out because, before they got involved with drugs, they were polite, respectable parents. They installed values in me at a young age and taught me a thing or two. When I think about my parents now, I only think about the good times. The time when they both were young, beautiful and drug free. If a person were to go and talk to any of their friends today, they would tell you nothing but kind things about both of them.

I will certainly say I was definitely a product of my environment. I think anybody else would have been too if they had seen and been through all of the bullshit that I did, especially at such a young age. After the funeral proceedings were over and we had laid my father to rest, I immediately went to the dope house to get high.

I was gone and had lost all self-control. Every time I would get high, I could hear this voice in the back of my head saying, "You're going to have to stop man; you can't keep doing this to yourself!" It was my spirit talking to me. Now when I look back on it, I was in a battle, my flesh wanted that temporary satisfaction, but my spirit didn't. I was actually battling the demons that were inside of my head, they didn't want to let me go until I died or drove myself insane. As usual, my flesh would win the battle, but the war was not over.

I went over to the dope lady's house, knocked on her door and she let me in, we called her Miss B. She said, "I'm sorry to hear about your dad." I said, "Thank you!" Then I asked her to sell me a fifty dollar rock. Here I was an hour after burying my dad,who died of an overdose of heroin, getting ready to get high. I guess that saying was true like father, like son.

I stayed at her house and smoked all day until night fall, using the death of my father as an excuse. People were coming over to purchase drugs, but I didn't care if

84

they saw me or not, I just kept on smoking. As they would leave, I could hear Miss B say to them, "He just lost his father, he's going through it."

After I had run out of drugs and money, she would give me more because she knew I would make the money later on to pay her back. She was feeding it to me and I just kept on taking it. The drug had a hold on me and it wouldn't let me go. Again, that voice in my head would say, "You gotta get off this stuff man or we're going to die! I'm not going to let it take over you!" although it seemed like it already had. I ran out of coke again.

I asked Miss B for one more hit, she said, "This is going to be the last one, after this you're going to have to chill out!" Then she handed me another rock. I was high as a kite and the voices would come back and say, "Man, you're killing yourself, you are going to end up dead like your father and aunt if you don't stop!" I would look around to see where these voices were coming from, but I couldn't find them because they were in my head, I was paranoid and hallucinating.

I finally ran out of coke and Miss B said, "Ray, you've had enough. You have to stop baby, it's time for you to come down!" She went to the cabinet and pulled out a bottle of Remy Martin. She poured me a large cup and said, "Drink this, it will make you come down."

I took two big swallows and after about ten minutes I could feel myself slowly coming down. We started talking and I just opened up and told her about everything, my break up, getting dismissed from the Navy and anything else that I could talk about, the cocaine had me rumbling out of my mouth. When I arrived at Miss B's house earlier that afternoon, after my father's funeral, I had a suit and tie on, looking real fresh and clean, but when I left her house later that night, the suit was all wrinkled up from my sweating, and my tie was loose around my neck. I looked like a bum who was still trying to be cool.

I pulled myself together after the Remy had brought me down. I left the dope house and went home, by then it was midnight, I had been smoking all day. As I was crossing the parking lot, some of the young drug dealers that I knew ran up to me and asked if I needed anything, meaning coke. I was surprised because they had never asked me before.

The cat was now out of the bag, everyone knew that I was smoking dope now. When I made it home, still tweaking, I went up the stairs to check on my mother to see how she was doing. Her door was closed, but I could hear voices. I knocked on the door and called out, "Momma, are you alright?" She said, "Yes, I am La Ray." I said, "Open the door." My mom replied, "No Ray, I'm busy." I could tell by her voice that she was in there getting high. My mother had weaned herself off of the prescription pills and started doing crack, thanks to me for bringing some over to the house a while ago.

It's a fucked-up feeling knowing that I introduced my own mother to crack cocaine, especially since I hated drugs so much when I was a child. How could this be? To this day I can't figure that one out. I knocked on the door again because I wanted to get some more. My mother said, in a more stern voice, "Leave me alone La Ray, I'm busy and I mean it!" I knew she was serious, so I left her alone to deal with the death of my father the way I did, by smoking cocaine.

I went into my room and laid on the bed staring at the ceiling while thinking about my father and how he died doing drugs, wondered whether it would happen to me. My flesh wanted more coke, but my spirit would fight back hard and resist the temptation. Tossing, turning and wondering what I was going to do with the rest of my life, I finally fell asleep.

CHAPTER 6

Change in My Life

The next morning I woke up with a pounding headache from smoking so much cocaine the previous night. I heard a knock at the front door and looked at the clock. It was 8:30 in the morning, I wondered who in the hell could this be knocking at my door so damn early in the morning. I wiped my eyes and went downstairs to see who it was.

To my surprise, when I opened the door it was two of my old high school friends, Bruce Hadley and Neil Windham. Although we lived in the same projects, we never hung out together because they weren't into drugs and all that street bullshit like I was.

I said, "What's up?" but in the back of my mind I was wondering why they were here. They both said, "What's up James?" We shook hands and Bruce said, "We're sorry to hear about your pops." "Thanks man!" I replied, still curious as to why they were at my house so early. They were some square ass niggas doing their college thing, playing football and shit.

Bruce asked, "Do you mind if we come in brother?" Now my curiosity began to grow even more because why would they want to come into my house, knowing the type of shit that I was into? I said, "Yeah, come in," but I was telling myself, "if they aren't talking about some dope or making some money, I don't want to hear shit they got to say." I asked, "What are y'all doing up so early?" I was trying to start a conversation. I knew something was up because these two guys wouldn't be at my house at 8:30 in the morning.

Bruce said, "Why are you letting yourself go like this brother? You were popular in high school playing football, had all the ladies and everything, we always looked up to you, now you're involved in drugs and stuff. That's not the James we know." I said, "Yeah, that was back in the days."

He replied, "Man, we're up at West Los Angeles Junior College running things, our coach asked us if we knew any other players from Venice High who wanted to play football and we thought about you. I know you still got that speed and those hands?" When he said that, I

89

swear to God I thought to myself, "I must still be high and this cocaine is undoubtedly starting to fuck with me."

I said, "Bro, that was two years ago, I'm older now. The hood done took me under and y'all know what I'm talking about." They knew about my drug situation and my getting dismissed from the Navy, so I didn't have to pull a front on them. I had to give them respect though, because they were trying to reach out to me on the positive side and, at that time, no one else was.

I said, "I'm going to keep it real with you, y'all tripping. I just got through smoking cocaine last night, and have been for the last year and a half. My pops just died, I got dismissed from the military, I'm in no shape to get out on no damn football field!" Although football has always been my passion, I had given up on it after high school and the Navy, especially when the coke game came in. I had never given it any more thought.

Neil then said something that kind of shocked me because he was a real quiet type of guy. "Bro, you don't have anything to lose, you are going to mess around and get killed fucking around out here in these projects!" He was right, I was on the border line and could go either way at any time.

I said, "Man, why are you guys coming over here trying to put all these silly ass thoughts in my head? It's too early to be hearing all this bullshit." Bruce replied, "God loves you and we do too. He sent us over here today to pray and talk to you, do you mind if we pray with you before we leave?"

In my mind I knew I needed prayer. My grandmother brought us up as Christians, I always believed in God, and if I ever needed him in my life, now was the time, so I let them pray for me. We held hands, bowed our heads and Bruce began to pray, "Dear Heavenly Father, we ask you, in Jesus' name, that you deliver us from all of our sins. We have all sinned and fallen short of the glory of God, we ask again, in your son Jesus' name, that you deliver James from all his addictions, short comings and troubles. We thank you Lord for waking us up this morning and to be able to share in the spirit with our brother James, in Jesus' name we pray." We all said, "Amen!"

I'm not going to lie, I felt something go through my body. It was as if a weight was lifted off my shoulders. I thanked them for coming over, we did a group hug, and they made their way to the front door. Before they walked out, Bruce turned and said, "You're going to play football again, God has already spoken it. We will be here waiting for you, brother!" Then they left.

After they were gone, I sat there wondering, Why me? Why is all this shit happening to me? I was too far gone.

I was convinced it would take a miracle for me to get off drugs let alone get me to step onto the football again.

My mom came downstairs and asked, "Who was that?" I said, "It was a couple of my old friends." She walked into the kitchen and to get something to eat.

I looked at her and wished that I had my old mother back. The lady that stood waiting with a smile on her face to surprise me with the toy she had hidden behind her back.

Not a day went by when I didn't have those thoughts; I would look at her and think about the past and how pretty she used to be. Her skin was cocoa brown, soft and smooth, but now she was scared up from falling down so much when she used to be high on the prescription pills, but who was I to judge? I was no better. . I loved her so much, I didn't care what she did, just as long as she didn't leave my sister and me.

I went upstairs and fell back asleep. I would sleep all day; night time would come. That's when all the smokers would come out. Sleep all day, up all night hustling, that was the life of a smoker, we were like vampires.

I had another homeboy named Billy. On the streets we called him, " Billy Hook" because of the shape of his head. He was a local drug dealer. I needed to make some quick cash to give to my mother for rent, buy some food, and of course, to get high. As long as I wasn't pushing a basket, collecting aluminum cans, and bottles and kept my weight up, I thought that I was okay. I called Billy's house and he answered the phone. I said, "What's up cuz? This is Smiley." Billy replied, "Smiley, what's up nigga?" "Nothing much Cuz." He then said, "I'm sorry to hear about your pops!" I replied, "Thanks man, he's in a better place now. I need a favor from you." "What do you need? You know I got you cuz." "Man, I need you to front me some dope, I have to make some money to help moms out!"

All the street niggas I dealt with always had respect for me, and would give me anything I asked for. I don't know if they were scared of me because of my past, or what, but they had the utmost respect for me, regardless of what my situation was. Billy said, "Cool I got you, but I'm going to have to go with you and show you how to sell this shit, cuz. I know this is your first time selling."

He was right, I had never sold crack before. It's totally different from selling marijuana, there's more money involved. Crack sells faster and you need to have someone watching your back for the jackers and police. Besides, he knew I was smoking, and I don't think he trusted me alone with his dope. This way I could make some money and have something to smoke on.

We went out that night to a spot in the projects called "Cocaine Corner." It was a cul-de-sac where people would come to buy their crack, then they would be gone as if it were a drive thru. The crazy part about it was that there would be people from all races and different parts of the city coming to purchase crack, and not just people who lived in the projects. Cars such as BMW's, limousines and even guys in their work trucks, would come through to purchase coke. One thing was for sure, crack did not discriminate.

When we got to the cul-de-sac, other dealers were already out there getting their hustle on. It was just as if it were the stock market, we had to under bid our competitor and still try to make a profit. At first it was all good because we were out there serving the customers, the money was coming in real fast, faster than I could count it.

I would make sure it was a 20, 50 or 100 dollar bill before stuffing it into one of my pockets.

After about an hour of selling dope, four unmarked police cars came speeding around the corner, heading right towards us. Some of the dealers took off running like jack rabbits, which is what I should have done, but I just stayed there and tried to stash my dope under the wheel of a car. Meanwhile, Billy was watching inside of the next car over. Billy had laid his seat all the way back and the police couldn't see him because it was dark. If I would have been as smart as Billy, I would have done the same thing. However I wasn't, the police caught me bending down and stashing drugs under the car, they jumped out with their guns drawn and ordered everyone who didn't run onto the ground. Suddenly a helicopter came out of nowhere and put the spotlight on us and made the whole block light up as if it was daytime.

The cops went straight to where I had hidden the dope and one of them said, "Well, well, look what we have here!" as he pulled the bag of crack from under the car. To my dismay, they never saw Billy in the other car. That's just how slick he was, he had the dope game down to a science. I was new to selling; I had panicked and got caught.

They arrested me, and two other dealers, for possession of sale of crack cocaine and took us to the Pacific Division Substation, where I stayed for about three days until I went to court, because I didn't have the money to bail out.

I couldn't afford a real lawyer, so the court appointed me a public defender.

The public defender came into the holding cell and said, "Mr. Soil, your bail is $20,000, you need $2,000 cash, which is ten percent, to bail out. Can you get it?" I said, "No, I don't have that kind of money."

"Your only option is to cop a plea deal and plead no contest. That's just another way of saying you're guilty without you actually saying that you committed the crime. That will get you six months in the L.A. County Jail, but you would do no more than six months because it's over crowded." He continued to say "Or we could take it to trial, but if you lose you're looking at two to three years in prison, and you're going to lose because the police officer saw you stashing the drugs!"

Back then, for some reason, a person would get more time for crack cocaine, even if it weighed the same as powder. I would find out later that it was because blacks would more than likely have crack, whereas the white boys had the powder.

I told the public defender that I would take the plea deal. We went before the judge who said, "Mr. Soil, you have been charged with distribution and selling crack cocaine, which is a felony in the state of California, how do you plead, sir?" I said, "No contest your Honor." "I hereby sentence you to six months in the L.A. County Jail, you will also be on one year of supervised probation and complete a two-month drug class, is that understood, sir?" I replied, "Yes sir, your Honor!" He hit the gavel and called the next case.

The sheriff escorted me out of the courtroom to another holding cell, where I would wait, along with the other prisoners, for the county jail bus to arrive. When the bus came, the correctional officers handcuffed all of us on a long chain. I felt as if I were a slave getting aboard a slave ship.

On the bus heading to the county jail, I finally had time to think. I thought about my whole life up until that point, how I had fucked it all up and everything that I had lost because of drugs. I didn't want to be found dead at the side of some apartment building, like my father, or roaming the streets like a bum, so I figured, at that time, jail was probably the best place for me to be.

When a person goes to jail everything stops. There's no more partying, doing drugs, running around in the streets and drinking. They sit around all day and do absolutely nothing, but think about what they did to get there, and how they never wanted to come back. That's just what I did, I even thought about the visit I had gotten from Bruce and Neil, just days before, and the seed they had planted in my head about playing football again.

When we arrived at the county jail, the gate was opened to allow the bus to pull in. All I could see were enormous black and white buses lined up, waiting to unload prisoners from all around Los Angeles County. African-Americans, Mexicans, Caucasians, bloods, crips, bums, women, homosexuals, child molesters and every other type of criminal you could imagine were getting off those buses.

After we were all processed in, the deputies gave us two county blue jumpsuits, a bedroll and a hygiene kit, then escorted us to the dorms. When I arrived at my assigned dorm, I immediately saw some of my Crip homeboys from Venice, a guy called S Loc and my other homeboy named Big Nut.

They said, "Smiley! What the hell are you doing in here? The last we heard you was in the Navy, what happened, cuz?" I was embarrassed because these guys had looked up to me, I felt as if I had let them down, which I had, because I was now incarcerated just like them.

I said, "Man, that Navy shit didn't work out for me. When I got out, I just started hustling and smoking cocaine, they caught me in projects with about twenty rocks and gave me six months." S Loc said, "You're going to do three to five months on that shit, cuz, you can do that standing on your head!"

Then he said, "We're fighting a hot one, they trying to get us for the murder of them Mexicans that got killed at the liquor store!" Big Nut said, "It's an empty bunk over here by us, grab your shit and come on!"

We grabbed my bedding, and all the county stuff they gave me, and made our way to where their bunks were. There's one thing about being from Venice, you're going to see some of your homeboys in jail, no matter which one they send you to.

The L.A. County Jail was like one massive dungeon where everything and everyone were separated by race. It had phones that only African-Americans used; the

Mexicans and Caucasians had their own phones as well. The toilets, showers, and dining area were separated by race. If a person crossed over and used another race's space or phone, there would be a straight-out riot.

After I got situated, and learned all of the jail house rules, I started jailing or programming, as it was often referred to. I started doing sit-ups, pushups and eating everything that I could get my hands on to get my weight back up. When a person is out there on the streets running around chasing dope, they don't eat right and lose a lot of weight.

A month went by and I could feel my body changing back to its old self again. Not only did I feel good, but I had picked up weight because the cocaine was out of my system. I also started going to church, reading the bible, trying to figure out my life's purpose, and what I was going to do when I got out of jail. After all, I was going to be on probation for a year. I had to take drug classes, piss in a bottle and if I screwed up, I would have to do two-to-three years in prison, that was not going to happen.

My public defender was right, nearly three more months had past when, and I was about to be released from the County Jail, due to the overcrowding. My flesh had the urge to get high as soon as I got home, but that little voice inside the back of my head said, "No, you have been clean for almost four months, you can't go back to that lifestyle anymore, leave the drugs alone." Besides, I had probation and those classes to attend; I couldn't fuck up, I had to stay strong, stick by my guns, and fight it.

When it was time for me to be released, the sheriff came to my cell and asked, "Are you James Soil?" I replied, "Yes sir!" He looked at my wristband to verify that it was me and said, "You have an early release, come with me." As we left the cell he continued down the corridor, calling other prisoners' names who were about to be released. After he had gotten about ten of us, he said, "Gentlemen, keep your hands inside your pockets and your shoulders against the wall, I don't want to hear any talking or I'm going to put your asses back in the cell and you can wait for the next shift!"

He led us to another part of the jail where our clothes waiting for us in green, meshed bags. He then said, "When I call your name, come and get your bag, and get dressed. The quicker we do this, the quicker you can go home." He started calling names. The deputy called my name, checked my wrist band again, threw me my bag of clothes, and told me to get dressed. He also said my ride was waiting on me, I was dumb founded because I had not called anyone for a ride.

I was excited and ready to get the hell out of the Los Angeles County Jail, I was also curious to see who had come to pick me up. I got dressed quickly, the deputy then put us in another tank, along with even more guys who were also being released. There must have been at least 300 people waiting to go home.

All of a sudden another sheriff opened the other door and said, "Gentlemen, when you hear your name, come to the front and show me your wristband, the faster we do this, the quicker you get out!" He started calling names, this process went on for like it seemed forever, then he finally called my name, "James Soil!" I said, "Right here, sir!" and made my way to the front. He looked at my wristband, cut it off with scissors, opened the other door and said, "Put your hands in your pockets and walk this way!"

We walked down this long, piss smelling tunnel with dimmed lights and graffiti sprawled all over it from what seemed like every gang, criminal and person that ever came through there. When they opened the last door, the brightness of the sunlight burst through. I shielded my eyes and could feel the warmth of the sunshine all over my face. Smelling that fresh air let me know that I was finally a free man again.

Although I had only spent four months in the county jail, it seemed as if I had been there forever. I had been to jail before, but that was the longest I have ever spent, and that was my first time going to the Los Angeles County Jail. I looked around trying to see who it was that had come to pick me up. I was thinking it would be my sister, but to my surprise, it was Bruce and Neil. I would have never imagined that these two guys would be there to pick me up, but there they were with huge smiles on their faces.

We hugged and I said, "Man, you guys didn't have to come and get me. I was going to catch the bus just as long as I was out of that fucking hell hole." Bruce said, "It's cool man, we just came to get you, so that we could talk with you again before you hit the streets. We went over to your mother's house and she told us she had been calling up here all week for your release date. She finally got in touch with somebody and they told her that you were getting out today, and she asked if we would pick you up."

I said, "That was cool of ya'll, good looking out." Neil said, "I know you want some real food, let's get something to eat." I said, "Hell yeah man, I want a fat and juicy cheeseburger, a cold soda and some chili fries from Fat Burgers, that food in the County Jail was fucked up!"

On the way to Fat Burgers I thanked them again for picking me up, then I said something that would surprise them as well. I said "Man, I thought about what y'all said about the school and the football thing, I was thinking about giving it a try." Neil turned around astonished, and said, "Now that's what I'm talking about, you should. It will be easy for you to check into West L.A. Just hang with us, we'll get you right in!"

In the back of my mind I had doubts, but my heart was pushing me to do it. I said, "I've been out of school for almost two-and-a-half years, man, it's going to be hard for me just to get into that everyday routine again, especially after all the shit I been through." Bruce then said, "It's not like high school, you only have about three-to-four classes a day and you are going to be on the football team, schools give you credit for that when you transfer."

"Transfer where?" I asked. They both said at the same time, "To a university, fool!" I said, "Y'all tripping now, no university is going to recruit me," Bruce said, "Yes they will, if you get your freak on." That's what we use to say in high school when a person would do something spectacular on the football field. I just sat there thinking, "These guys have more faith in me then I have in myself."

We pulled into Fat Burgers and ordered our food. When the cashier gave us our food, I was like a mad man tearing into the bag to get my burger. The first bite was delicious, I finished it within two minutes, not saying a word until I was done eating.

After we ate, they dropped me off at my mother's house. Bruce jokingly said, "You should come and throw the ball around with us some time and show us some of them old moves, I have an extra pair of cleats you can have." I replied, "Cool, just let me know when ya'll coming through." Bruce replied, "We'll let you know, just be ready." We shook hands and they drove off.

As I made my way to my mother's house, I said to myself, "Don't lead these guys on, if you're not going to do it, then don't." There's one thing about me, once I make up my mind to do something, I'm going to do it. I had my mind more than half-way made up.

When I opened the door to my mother's apartment, Carolyn, my mom and another lady, who I didn't know, were sitting at the table with their bibles out, having what

105

looked like a bible study. I said, with a smile, "Hi Mom, I'm home!" She jumped up and hugged me real tight and said, "My baby's home, thank you Jesus!"

Then Carolyn came over, hugged me and introduced me to the other lady. She said, "This is Miss Mildred, she is one of the ushers at the church." I said, "Hello," and shook her hand. Miss Mildred said, "Hi young man, welcome home."

I don't know why it was, but it seemed as if there was something different about my mother, she looked more upbeat and happier, it was as if she had a glow about herself. I was expecting to come home and see her either on a drug binge or coming down from one, but that wasn't the case, she looked content and I hadn't seen her look like that in a long time.

My mother asked, "Did Bruce pick you up? He's been calling all week to see when you were getting out." I said, "Yeah, him and Neil picked me up." My mother asked, "Are you hungry?" I replied, "No thank you, we stopped and got something on the way home!"

We talked for a while about my future plans. I told her I was finished with drugs and that I was going to try to turn my life around, I could tell from her expression she had her doubts, but my mind was already made up. I went upstairs to take a real shower.

It felt good to be home. I realized that doing cocaine again would not be the answer for me, I didn't want to get out of jail and start doing it all over again. I had my weight up and wanted a fresh new start. Although I had been through a lot and lost everything, I was only going on 21-years old; I could get it all back and then some. I had just spent four months in jail, clean and sober, it didn't make any sense to get out and start that vicious cycle of smoking crack again.

My plan was to see what was up with the junior college that Bruce and Neil were talking about, they honestly had me thinking about it. If I were going to try and change my life, this would be my last opportunity to do so. I stayed in the shower, for what seemed like hours, thinking about my future and washing the filth from the county jail off of me. Cocaine was a mental addiction, not a physical addiction like heroin. I could fight it if I could block cocaine out of my mind. On the other hand, when a person gets hooked on heroin, they have to have it or they will get physically sick and go through withdrawals, it's called "cold turkey."

The first day out was the hardest. It's funny how a person gets out of jail clean and sober, yet as soon as they get out, people want to get them dirty again

My so-called "friends" found out I was out of jail and called me on the very same night, saying, "Come on over, I got a blast for you." A "Blast" is lingo for a big hit of coke to get a person started again. I was both amazed and hurt when I got those phone calls. I said to myself, "These guys don't give a fuck about me, they're trying to see me down and out, whereas guys like Bruce and Neil are trying to uplift me, and give me motivation to go to college."

I was seriously starting to lean towards the school and football thing. I began to dream again. After showering, I put on some fresh clothes, grabbed the keys to my mother's car and drove around the corner to my sister's house. She had just gotten married to this guy named Hampton; they had moved into their new house. I wanted to see it and surprise her at the same time.

My sister had tried drugs a while back, when I had brought it to the house for the first time, but it wasn't her thing, it didn't do anything for her. It's strange how cocaine had a different effect on people, some people could take a hit and just walk away from it, while others would hit it and their whole personality would change.

I arrived at my sister's house, knocked on the door and she opened it. Her face lit up when she saw me, she said, "Hey boy, they finally let you out!" She gave me a loving hug and told me to come in. I said, "Your house is nice!" Tonnetta replied, "Thank you, God is good." She was cooking some fish and it smelled good. "I know you're hungry from eating that nasty jailhouse food." I replied, "I just ate a couple of hours ago, but I can't turn down your tasty catfish."

My sister and I had a real cool relationship, even though she could get crazy sometimes. Her zodiac sign was cancer; she would get mad at your ass if you pushed the wrong buttons. I remember when we were younger, I was teasing her about something, she turned around out of nowhere, hit me with a bottle of soda and knocked my tooth out. My mom whipped her ass good because I didn't want to hit her, after that I never teased her again.

She made me a plate of fish and we sat down and talked. Tonnetta said, "So, what are you going to do now that you're out? I know you're not going to start smoking that stuff again?" I said, "Naw, I'm done with that shit. I'm just going to take it one day at a time. Bruce and Neil

109

are trying to get me to go to West L.A. Junior College; they came and picked me up from jail." She said, "That was polite, you should go to school up there with them, I heard they're doing good. You need to hang around some positive people, so you can stay clean and out of trouble."

I could talk to my sister about anything, I knew in my heart that she would always be there for me no matter what. She then asked, "What's momma over there doing?" "Her, Carolyn and some other lady named Miss Mildred were over having bible study or something." I said, "Yeah, momma been trying real hard to leave them drugs alone, she's been going to church and everything." Tonnetta replied, "That's good. I knew it was something different about her, she seemed as if she was more at peace."

I felt good when my sister told me my mom was trying to kick her drug habit, now, if I just stayed strong, we could leave the drugs alone all together. I finished my plate, we talked a little while longer, then it was time for me to go. I wanted to go see some of my other homeboys in Venice to let them know that I was out. We hugged each other, when I got up to leave. She said, "Be strong, I love you brother!" I replied, "I love you too and I will."

I left her house, heading down to the hood where my true test would come. The block was hot and drugs were everywhere. If I ever were going to beat this thing I would have to fight it head on, not try to run and hide from it.

CHAPTER 7

Goodbye My Friend

When I got down to Venice, I was driving around hitting blocks to see what was up. The first person I saw from afar was my homeboy World. I said to myself, "Let me go and surprise this nigga and see what he is up to." I drove up to where he was. As I got closer to him, I could see that he was bent over, as if he was throwing up or something.

I quickly put the car in park, jumped out and said, "World, what's going on?" He said, "Smiley, pat my back, cuz, pat my back!" He was gagging like he had swallowed something. "The police just came by and I had to swallow my rocks, pat my back cuz!" Spit was coming out of his mouth; he was steadily gagging. I started patting his back harder and he began spitting up white cocaine rocks, a lot of them. I said, "Damn cuz, you could have overdosed on all that shit!" He said again, "Them motherfucking police came out of the alley on my ass; I had to swallow them!"

Back then, the dealers would keep the rocks inside their mouth just for that purpose. When a person would come to purchase the dope, they would just take a rock out of their mouth, and sell it to them covered with spit and all. Now that I look back on it, a person had to be a serious dope fiend to smoke something a nigga just took out of his mouth, let alone out of; their ass. The dealers kept rocks there too, they called it "keystering."

World was starting to look really awful; I could see the drugs were taking a toll on him.

Being locked up for those few months helped to clear my head and allowed me to see the harsh and negative affect crack was having on the community, the people and myself.

No matter what, World and I always maintained our appearances, but now my homebody was looking tired and worn down.

Regardless of his addiction, World was still my best friend. He had let me stay with him at his family's apartment when my family and I were evicted from our house, and I needed a temporary place to live. As he picked up the rocks from off of the ground, he asked me the question that I had heard a few times already upon my release. He said, "Cuz, let's go take a blast; You just got out of jail, nigga, I know you want to get high."

I replied, "Man they got me on probation and shit, I can't even fuck around with it anymore." World said, "I heard that, Smiley, I'm not mad at you, I wish I could shake this shit, but it just won't let me." I replied, "You can man, you just have to take it one day at a time, you think that shit don't be calling me?" World responded by saying, "Give me a ride around the corner, this nigga owes me some money!" I replied, "Cool, hop in man!" We got into the car and I took him around the corner.

It was one of the old crack houses, where we used to smoke dope, I knew he was going in there to get high, but there was nothing that I could say or do, World was going to do his own thing anyway.

Sadly enough, that would be the last time I would see my homeboy, and best friend, Tony "World" Freeman alive again. A week later he was killed whilst fleeing from the police. The cops were chasing him on his motorcycle when He turned the corner too wide, while driving too fast, lost control and crashed into a brick wall, breaking almost every bone in his body.

World's death was a blow to the community and to me. Although he had a drug problem, he was a real smart and genuine person that was still loved by everyone. World was best known for being a Jailhouse lawyer because when he was in jail, he would spend most of his time studying in the law library, trying to help people get out of prison by finding loopholes in their transcripts. He even beat a case while acted as his own lawyer at his trial. Thus, he got the name "World "because he came from the streets, but he knew a lot about the world. I love him to this day and I will never forget him.

I was one of the pallbearers at the funeral. I had never done that before and carrying my best friend in a casket was something that I will never forget. After putting him into the hearse, the procession caravanned to the graveyard and we laid him to rest. As people slowly started to leave, I stayed until I was the last one there, just sitting there and crying.

All I thought about was the good times we had shared together, how we would go over to his house and listen to Michael Jackson's Off the Wall album. At that time, we had both been in love with our high school sweethearts, we played it over and over while chilling, thinking about our girls.

We would go get our Jheri Curls together; World had hipped me to this beauty shop in Los Angeles called, "Sir

James" where they did hair really good. We would get our hair done and go straight to Fox Hills Mall and walk around as if we were stars. Girls would come up to us and ask, "Who are you guys/? And where y'all from?" We would say, "Venice Sho-Line!", that was the name of our hood, and we just kept on strolling.

World would come to all my high school football games to pump me up saying, "You gotta get yours tonight, Smiley!" He also had this big charming smile that would draw people towards him.

With the passing of my father, and now my best friend, I knew I had to make a change in my life—going back to school and playing football again was my only option.

I finally pulled myself together and went home. Even though I had the urge to smoke some dope, I couldn't. I had to fight those demons that day and in the days to come.

The next morning I heard a knock at the door. I went downstairs to see who it was and by my surprise, it was Bruce and Neil. Bruce held up a pair of football cleats in my face and said, "Are you ready?" They had caught me totally off guard, I said, "Man, y'all just don't give up." Bruce replied, "We told you that we were coming, Bro.

We're sorry to hear about Tony." I said, "Thanks, that was my boy."

These guys were a trip, they were genuinely trying to reach out to me and help change my life. I guess they figured all I needed was a push, they knew I had a lot of potential and they simply didn't want to see me waste it. I needed a push; I thought about what my sister had said about how I needed to start hanging out with more positive people, I guess they were the ones.

I invited them in and said, "Let me put on some shorts and I'll be right down." I went up the stairs to wash my face and brush my teeth. I found some shorts and pulled out my old high school football jersey. When I put the jersey on, I could feel myself getting pumped up, I said to myself, "Fuck it, this is the beginning of your new life." I put my game face on and went downstairs. When I got downstairs, Bruce and Neil were looking at me kind of strange. I think when they saw me with my old jersey on it threw them for a loop. I said, "Let's do it!" and we went outside.

The projects had a lot of space and grass, this would be our makeshift practice field. It was a beautiful morning, the sun was shining and the grass had just been cut, so it was nice and even. The smell of the fresh green grass had me feeling ready to play, but when we started to stretch, I began to have second thoughts. I started questioning myself and wondering if I still had it. Or if it was all a tremendous waste of time.

Bruce started talking shit, saying, "You think you can still hang? We can start off slow if you want, I don't want you to pull a muscle or anything?" That was one of the things I loved about football, the shit talking and playing mind games with your opponent. Who's the fastest, who can catch better, you can't stop me, the intimidation, who's the hardest hitter, it was all done in a fun and competitive manner. I said to Bruce, "This is what I do, dog. It's like riding a bike, you never forget!" I was ready to see if I still had it or if the drugs had taken away all of my ambitions and my will.

Neil started to instigate, saying, "I'm going to quarterback, you niggas go one on one." I loved playing football, but I was what they call in sports an "Underachiever." For those of you who don't know what that is, it's a person who has all the athletic abilities, speed, size, skills and power but does nothing with it. I was all of the above, but I had chosen to run the streets, instead of running on the football field.

If you have ever seen a young, six-foot-eight brother in the hood, smoking dope and walking around like bum, instead of on the basketball court, that's an underachiever. They were blessed with the size and talent, should be in college or the pros, but unfortunately, they chose the street life. There are a lot of young brothers like that around the country, in the hoods and inside the penitentiary.

An "Overachiever," on the other hand, is a guy five-foot-two, 150 pounds wet, but will slam dunk on your ass, or run an 80 yard punt return as if it were a walk in the park. I tried to go both ways, it didn't work for me, but that day, for some reason, I felt as if I was the man.

I knew Bruce and Neil thought that I was a little washed up, I was getting ready to show them the new James Soil. After we stretched out, and threw the ball around for a while, I was ready to do my thing. Bruce said, "Come on, James, show me what you got!" He threw me a pass, I caught the ball with my fingertips and could feel my fingers sink into the Pigskin as I caught it. I loved that feeling. My confidence grew more as I caught the ball; I knew my technique was still there.

Then Bruce said, "You go first at wide receiver, I will cover you. Be careful now, I don't want you to hurt yourself!" I just smiled at him; Neil and me huddled up to

119

call a play. He asked, "What are you going to run?" I immediately said, "A stop and go." It's a route a receiver runs at full speed, for about six yards, stops on a dime and then turns around. The quarterback pumps the ball as if he's going to throw it, but he doesn't. This makes the defensive back over commit, and when he does, the receiver turns back around sprinting up the field. It's a timing pattern and I mastered it.

Neil said, "Cool, on two!" We clapped hands and I stepped to scrimmage line; Neil started calling the signals, I looked Bruce in the eyes, I was getting ready to burn him on the first play, so I could stop his shit talking.

Neil yelled, "Ready, set, hut, hut!" I took off like a rocket, kicking up grass behind me as I ran towards Bruce at full speed. When I got to about six or seven yards, I planted my foot, stopped on a dime and turned around. Neil pumped the ball, Bruce over committed as planned, came up, took the bait, and I turned around, heading up the field like a track star. Bruce tried to recover, but it was too late, I had one step on him, and that's all I needed. Neil threw the ball deep, I looked up, saw the blue sky, and a brown spiraling football floating in the air. Suddenly, everything slowed down and got quiet, all I could hear was the wind blowing and Bruce and I breathing heavily, he was right on my hip.

As the ball began to descend, I made my move. I was taught, throughout my years of playing football, to always catch the ball at its highest point, back then I could slam dunk a basketball as well. I jumped up to catch the ball, it felt as if I were flying, I stretched out my arms, and the ball sunk into my fingertips. I had jumped so high that when I looked down, I was actually riding on Bruce's shoulder. I pulled the ball in, Bruce hit the ground with me landing on top of him.

I looked back at Neil, he had his hand over his mouth and a look of disbelief. He yelled, "DAMN, JAMES, THAT WAS A COLD ASS CATCH, I'M NOT GOING TO LIE!" I got up, spiked the ball and said to Bruce, "Yeah, nigga, now what, now what!" I was the shit talker now.

Bruce got up smiling and saying, "Damn James, you still got it, man!" He shook my hand. Football was my passion, I loved it! I could spin the ball on my finger like a basketball and do all kinds of other tricks with it. As I said earlier, I was an "Underachiever." That one catch would send me on my way back to the sport I loved so much as a kid, and push me even further away from drugs. We continued to run patterns against each other, I don't know what, why, or how, but something got into me that day, and I came out on top.

From that day on, Bruce, Neil and I created a new bond with each other. We would work out every other day, lifting weights, running routes and preparing for the upcoming football season. I had made up my mind that I would enroll in West Los Angeles Junior College. It was almost the end of summer, if I wanted to play I would have to go up there and enroll as soon as possible.

I told my mother I was going back to school, she said, "For what?" "To play football!" I replied. She then said, "Boy, that's just a pipe dream, you need to find a job!" Although she was back and forth with her addiction, drugs made my mother mean sometimes, after she would come down or when she ran out, she would just become this evil person and say hurtful things.

At times I would have doubts and say to myself, "Maybe you should just find a job and hang up your cleats for good," but I couldn't. My mind was already made up. I had been clean from drugs going on almost five months now and attending those drug classes was starting to help me even more. Listening to other people tell their stories made me realize that I was not the only one trying to kick his drug habit and turn over a new leaf. The urges would come and go because, living in the projects, I was still around coke, my mother and some of her other friends were doing it at the house from time to time, but for now, I was being strong and holding on. It was still going to be an uphill battle.

Although I was inactive in the gang activity at the time, I would still go kick it with my little homeboys to keep my ears to the streets. Another Crip set had formed in the projects, families had moved from Venice, as we did, and slowly, but surely enough, had moved out there to start another gang. These guys were younger, crazier, and more deadly because of the rise of Crack cocaine. They were making a lot of money that allowed them to purchase Uzi's, Tech-nines, AK-47's and any other guns that they needed for protection. The Culver City Locos was the major Latina gang that ran the projects and didn't like the fact that the newly formed Crips were cutting into its drug profits.

One day, the young homies were hanging out in the front, sitting on the cars, just chilling. I said to them, "I'm getting ready to go to Mickey D's,"(that's what we called McDonald's in the hood, if yall want something, you better give me your money." Everybody started giving me their money to bring them something back.

After I had gathered all of the money together, my homeboy, Sonny Man, and me drove to Mcdonalds to order the food. We came back and started handing out everybody's food when, all of a sudden, this Mexican popped up from around the building and yelled out, "Culver City Locos fool!" And just started busting off shots, BANG, BANG, BANG, BANG!

I ran into the house, breathing hard from running for my life. My mother said, "Boy! Who's doing all of that shooting out there?" I said, "A Mexican started shooting at us, one of my boys started shooting back!" As I continued telling her what happened, I noticed a bullet hole in the bag, as I pulled out my Big Mac from out of the sack, a bullet had gone right through the middle of the Styrofoam container. I didn't say anything to my mother about how close I had come to getting shot because I shouldn't have been out there anyway, being that I was on probation anyway.

That would be the second time I had cheated death out there in those projects. The first time was when I was out there on drugs, curb serving in this other dealers spot. "Curb Serving" is when outsiders come to buy drugs, and a person takes their money to get the dope for them, and in return they give you some of their dope or a little money.

This young dope dealer named "Killa" came by and said, "This is my spot, nigga, get your smoking ass out of here!" Although I was out there smoking, I wasn't a punk ass nigga. I said to him, "Fuck you, little nigga, I'm out here trying to make some money, just like you, nobody owns shit around here!" He then said, "Alright then, nigga, if your ass is here when I come back, I'm going blow your motherfucking head off!" He left to go get his gun.

Some of the other dudes I was with said, "Come on, Smiley, let's just go somewhere else and get some sales, that little nigga is crazy and he's going to come back!" I said, "Fuck that shit cuz, I'm not running from any nigga!" Minutes later he came back with a gun stuffed down his pants, I could see the bulge. My boy said again, "Man just leave!" I had so much foolish pride, and I was trying to make some money to get high, I couldn't see myself running like a bitch, so I just stood there like a fool. He came walking up towards me, pulled out a 45 Caliber pistol and said, "Nigga, didn't I tell you to get your motherfucking ass out of my spot!" He aimed the gun right at my head, standing about ten feet away, God moved my head slightly to the left and Killa fired the gun. "Bang!" I felt the bullet skin my ear.

I just stood there, everyone else there was standing around, looking in amazement and shock that I was still alive. The guy was too because he was aiming to kill me, but thanks to God he missed. He kept the gun pointed at me and said, "Man just get your ass out of here!" I then walked away with my foolish pride still intact.

A week later Killa got shot in the eye in a drive-by shooting. Two months later he would be murdered in Los Angeles in a drug deal gone bad, I guess you can say that God does work in mysterious ways. The strange thing about Killa was that before his death he bought his own tombstone, picked out his casket, took pictures and wrote his own obituary. He had done so much evil shit out there in the streets that he knew the Grim Reaper was not far behind.

CHAPTER 8

Victory

When it was time to enroll at West Los Angeles Junior college, Bruce, Neil and me caught the bus to the campus. It was only 15 minutes away from the projects so that was cool.

We arrived on campus; I was surprised to see all the pretty girls that were enrolling that day. I said, "Man you guys see all these fine ass bitches in here?" "Wait until school starts, you haven't seen all of them yet," Bruce replied. As we stood in line, I started feeling better about my decision to return back to school, I had been drug-free for six months now and my self-esteem was getting higher.

The lady behind the counter said, "Next in line please." That would be me. I walked up to the counter and began my enrollment process. She said, "Hi, welcome to West Los Angeles Community College, we're happy to have you. May I see your I.D. please?" I handed her my I.D.

"I see this is going to be your first year here?" she said. "Yes, I'm kind of getting a late start," I replied. "You're never too old to learn," she said. That made me feel better.

After we had completed the enrollment process, she informed me that I had qualified for a PellGrant. I asked, "What is that?" She replied, "It's a non-repayable loan provided by the Government to help for your books, bus passes and other things you may need for you education, would you like to apply for it?" "Yes!" I replied. I was not going to turn down free money, going back to school may not have been a bad idea after all.

My fears about returning to school were all but gone now, all I had to do was make it onto the football team. She sent me to another building and told me the councilors would help me choose my required classes. After I finished enrolling in school, received all of my required classes, it was now time to meet the football coaches.

Bruce, Neil and me went down to the coaches' office. As we entered the office, Bruce said, "Hey coach, how's everything going? This is my friend James Soil, we went to Venice High together." He stuck out his hand and said, "Hi James, I'm Coach Babcock, this is my assistant, Coach Smith." I shook both of their hands, then Coach

Babcock asked, "What position do you play Soil?" I said, "wide receiver, defensive back and kick-off return." He replied, "Good, we need more players who can play multiple positions. Practice starts next week, see you then!" They shook my hand again and we left the office.

As we left the campus, and got back on the bus, I was surprised at how smooth and easy everything had turned out. I couldn't wait to get home to tell my mother I had just enrolled in community college. The bus dropped us off back at the projects and I rushed home to tell my mother about my day.

My mom was upstairs in her room when I arrived home. I said, in a happy voice, "Momma, I just finished enrolling at West Los Angeles Junior College!" Her response was, "That's good La Ray, but you are still going to have to get a job!" She went back to her room.

I was hurt because it seemed as if there were nothing I could do to make her proud of me. Since getting dismissed from the Navy, I felt as if I had let her down, but I always said to myself, "One day I'm going to make her proud of me again." I went into my bedroom to read all of the brochures and information I had received from school that day.

Our apartment was like a semi-crack house. Although drugs weren't being sold from out of there, people would come over almost every day to smoke cocaine. I knew this would make it even harder for me than ever before because the temptation was still there.

Football practice started two weeks before school. On the first day of practice I was extremely nervous because all the guys knew each other, I just knew Bruce and Neil. I felt like an outcast, I would have to earn my respect all over if I wanted to play football again!

After we stretched out and did our calisthenics, they split us up into positions, Bruce went with the defensive backs, Neil the defensive line and I went with the wide receivers. As we lined up to do our routes, the two superstars, Stephen Baker and Bruce Walker, were at the front of the line.

I watched as Stephen walked up to the scrimmage line; Coach Babcock shouted, "The first route is a post, keep your eye on Baker, he will show you how to run a proper post route!" I had noticed that Baker was a little frail, soft spoken guy about five-foot-eight, 160 pounds, but he was fast and had a lot of heart. He did a simple post pattern where the receiver runs up the field about eight yards, plants his foot and runs toward the goal post. He ran a perfect pattern, caught the ball and turned up field, Coach Babcock said, "God job Baker, that's how you run the post route."

Bruce Walker was next, he was a bigger receiver, about six-foot-two, 185 pounds. Bruce ran his post route real precise; he looked like a pro. After he ran his pattern, Coach Babcock said the same thing. After a couple of other guys had run their pattern, my turn was next. I was nervous and sweating bullets; I could feel that all eyes were on me.

I walked up to the scrimmage line, the quarterback started calling the signals, "Ready, set, hut." I took off running full speed down the field. After about eight yards, I planted my foot and headed towards the goal post, the quarterback released the ball and at that moment everything just slowed down. All I could hear was my breathing and my footsteps hitting the grass.

The ball was kind of high, it looked as if he were going to overthrow me. I jumped up, reached out with one hand extended in the air, and snatched the ball out of the air with my finger tips. Coach Babcock said, "That was an impressive catch Soil!" I could hear the chatter of the other guys saying, "Damn, did you see that?" and "Who is that?" As I ran back to get into line, all the guys were giving me high fives, and saying how good the catch I had made was.

At that point I had gained a little respect, but I still had a long way to go because Stephen Baker and Bruce Walker were already penciled in starters being heavily recruited by top universities, and they were not trying to share the spotlight.

After practice, guys were coming up to my locker talking to me and telling me how good that catch was I had made earlier, I started feeling like part of the team.

On the way home, I decided that I would go to the Fox Hills Mall to look for a job. I went inside the mall and started walking around the different stores filling out job applications. I found this one kids shoe store called "Buster Browns" and asked for a job application.

The Korean owner said, in broken English, "You looking for a job?" I said, "Yes, I'm in school and I need something part time." He gave me an application and said, "You fill this out and I give you job, okay?" I filled out the application and gave it back to him. He looked over it and said, "You come to work this time tomorrow, okay James? My name is Mr. Lee!" I replied, "Yes sir, thank you I will be here tomorrow!" We shook hands and I left the store.

I hopped on the bus in astonishment, I couldn't believe I had got a job so easily and couldn't wait to go home to tell my mother. When I arrived home, I went inside full of joy and said, "Momma, I got a job at the mall!" All she said was, "Good, now you can help me with some of these bills!" Then she went back into her room and closed the door.

Sometimes I would just trip off of my mother, it seemed as if I couldn't do anything to make her proud of me anymore and that truly hurt me. At times, when she would be in her Christian mode, she was fine, but when she would resort to her smoking mode she would change. I understood her split personality, I just wished for the day that she would stop doing drugs altogether, but at least she was trying.

I had it all figured out, I would go to school in the morning, go to practice after that, and then go to work in the evening. I knew it would be hard, but it was something I had to do because this routine would keep me busy and off of drugs.

School had not started yet, I was just practicing and working. My first day on the job went smoothly. Mr. Lee took me around the store, showed me the setup, he then took me into the back and showed me how to find the style and size of the shoes. It was very easy; I caught on fast. When a person stepped one foot into the store, I would make sure that they would not leave without buying a pair of shoes. I had the gift of gab, I would start up a conversation with customers, they would tell me what they were looking for, and I took care of them and their kids.

School was about to start, I couldn't sleep at all the night before, it felt as if I were starting elementary all over again, I had butterflies in my stomach. I was sincerely looking forward to starting my first day of class.

I woke up, took a shower, got dressed, and was out the door to meet Bruce and Neil at the bus stop, they were already there. We shook hands and Bruce asked, "Are you ready for your first day at West L.A., James?" I replied, "Hell yeah, I can't wait to see all of those beautiful girls!" Neil said, "Don't worry, you're going to see a lot of them today!" The bus came and we jumped on it, heading to our first day of school.

The bus dropped us off on campus. Just as Bruce and Neil said, it was nothing but pretty girls everywhere, I had never seen so many pretty black girls in one place before. As we walked onto campus, I could honestly say the guys were not lying about the girls, I had to get focused and remember what I had come there for. We went our separate ways to go to class.

West L.A. was like high school; who's the most popular, a fashion show, and full of cliques. I was older now and I knew that I had to stay away from all of that bullshit. I settled in pretty good, got through all of my classes, went to work, practice, then headed home to the projects, which I was beginning to hate more and more.

I hated even looking at the walls in the projects. Imagine sitting in your living room or bedroom, looking at painted-over cylinder blocks making up your walls. We had to use double sided tape to hang up pictures because we couldn't put nails through the cement. I hated that place and dreamed every day of escaping it; even outside, there was always something going on.

I remember one night I was awakened by the sound of a gunshot, "BANG!" I waited for about a minute before I went to see what happened. I pulled the curtain back real slow, all of a sudden I saw four people carrying somebody. They each had one limb, his head was bobbing back and forth, they dropped him right across from my apartment.

One of them ran into the house screaming, "CALL 911, CALL 911!" while the others were kneeling down

135

trying to comfort whoever it was that had got shot. I had seen many dead bodies before, but the way they were carrying him, I could tell that he was already dead. About five minutes later I could hear the sirens from the ambulance and fire trucks coming. I had a bird's eye view and watched the madness unfold.

I knew the family who lived across from me, but I couldn't tell if it were one of them who had been shot. I watched as the paramedics pumped on the mystery person's chest, they were working on him desperately while the people who were carrying him scrambled back and forth in a frenzy. I never went outside, I just watched from my window in silence. They put him on a stretcher and wheeled him away. I sat there watching for a little while longer then I slowly let the curtain go and went to get back into my bed. As I laid there, I wondered who had gotten shot and what had happened; knowing that I would find out the next morning. I said, "I hate this place!" And I fell back asleep.

The next morning came, I got dressed and left the house heading to the bus stop, they had yellow tape everywhere. Some detectives were out there were questioning people. When one of the detectives saw me coming out of the house, he said, "Excuse me sir, do you live there?" I replied, "Yes." Then he asked, "Did you hear any shooting last night?" I replied, "I hear shots every night, it's normal around here. I'm running late for school, I have to go!" He gave me his card and said, "My name is Detective Jones, if you have any information you can call me on this number." He handed me his business card, I took the card and left. As I got further away from the crime scene, I crumbled the card up, dropped it on the grass and made my way to the bus stop.

When I got to the bus stop, as usual, Bruce and Neil were already there. Bruce said, "That was fucked up what they did to little Chris last night, I know you heard the gunshots." I said, "Damn! That was little Chris? I was looking out the window and saw them carrying him. They dropped him in front of Biggs' house." Bruce then said, "They shot him in the face, it was them niggas from Grape Street Crips. He was out there selling dope and they called him to the car as if they wanted to buy something. When he walked up to the car they shot him then drove off!" I said, "Damn that was fucked up, that little nigga was only 15-years-old!"

The Grape Street Crips were another black gang from Watts that wanted some of the lucrative drug money that was being made inside the projects. Killing little Chris was one of their tactics to move the sub-gang from Venice out of the way. I had become numb to all of the bullshit that was happening in the projects, it happened so frequently it was as if we were living in the middle of a war zone, which we were, but it was a war zone for drug territory and money.

The bus came and we got aboard heading on our way to school. "What a way to start the day," I said to them as we rode the bus. Then Bruce asked, "Are you ready for the game Saturday, James?" I said, "Yep, but I doubt it if I play with Stephen Baker and Bruce Walker ahead of me!" Neil said, "Just be ready dog, you never know." I replied, "I will." The bus dropped us off and we went to our classes.

As I sat in class, I thought about what had happened the night before and about little Chris. He should be in class at high school this morning, instead of laying on a gurney in a freezer in some coroner's office. I looked around the classroom and said to myself, "These people don't have a clue about what I have been through in the past year and a half, or what I saw last night." They didn't know how fortunate they truly were. I pulled out my notepad, and a pen from my backpack. and began to take notes from the teacher's lecture while at the same time having flashbacks of what I saw the previous night.

Later on that day at practice everybody was getting hyped for the game against El Camino Real on Saturday. We had a good practice as a team, but individually I was not happy because I was not getting as many reps as I wanted to. In high school, I started every game, but now I would sit on the bench and have to cheer my team on from the sidelines. This would be a new experience for me, but, as we say in football, I had to suck it up. After practice the coaches handed out brand new blue and gold uniforms; they were sweet, we had our names on the back of the jersey. I had gotten the number four, I said to myself, "I might not play, but I'm going to be looking clean out there." One thing about playing football, you had to look good in your uniform, that was a must.

After practice, I took a shower and headed to work. I was about 15 minutes early that day and for some reason I was feeling good. It seemed as if I was finally getting my life together again. Even though my mother was still not impressed with me, I was, and that's all that mattered. When I arrived at Buster Browns, Mr. Lee was there, he saw that I was early, he had a smile on his face and said, "You here early today James?" I replied, "Yes sir, we had a short practice." We made small talk, then I got my first customer. A man and his little daughter walked in, I greeted them and let them look around the store.

After looking around at shoes for a while, the little girl saw a pair that she liked and said, "I want these shoes right here daddy!" He replied, "Ok honey, go show the salesman." I met them half way and said, "You found something you like?" The little girl replied, "Yes I like these!" she handed me the shoes. I said, "Those are pretty, you're going to look nice in those!" She smiled and said, "They are going to be my back to school shoes!" "Do you know what size you wear?" She replied, "A size three!" I said, "Take off your shoe and let me measure your foot just to make sure."

She took off her shoe and I measured her foot, "Three and a half, you grew a little bit!" "Yes!" she said with the cutest smile. Then her dad said, "We were here about three months ago and she wore a three." "They grow fast, let me go and get the shoes, I'll be right back," I replied. When I got up to go get the shoes, Mr. Lee was watching. He was smiling and gave me the thumbs up sign.

I returned quickly with the shoes and asked her to try them on. When she stood up, I pushed down on the tip of the shoe, as I had been taught, to see if she had enough room, then asked, "How does that feel?" "Good!" she said. "That means you want them?" Her father asked, she shook her head yes, with a smile on her face.

Her dad then said, "We'll take them, tell the man thank you." "Thank you!" she said"You're welcome!" I replied. I helped her take off the shoes and gave the box to Mr. Lee so he could ring them up. After he rang them up, I handed the little girl her bag, a sucker and they were on their way.

Mr. Lee said, "Very good James, you learning fast, you good salesman!" Little did Mr. Lee know that I was a hustler from the streets trying to change my life. This was another hustle, it was just legit. After I had made a dozen or more shoe sales that day, I impressed my boss Mr. Lee. It was time for me to take my break, Mr. Lee said, "James you go eat now, I watch the store!" I said, "Ok!" and went to   go   get   a   bite   to   eat.

CHAPTER 9

School Boy Crush

As I was walking to the food court, I saw this beautiful caramel skinned black girl, with a long ponytail, working behind the counter at Mrs. Fields Cookies. I stopped right there in my tracks and decided to get cookies. When I got in line she immediately went into the back room. "I must have scared her away," I said to myself.

About 30 seconds later she came back out with her hair down, looking even more gorgeous than before. I thought she was flirting with me. At that same time she looked me dead in the eyes and smiled. I was mesmerized; I had never in my life seen a girl in person, so beautiful before. I smiled back.

When it was my turn to order, she said, "What will you be having today?" I just stared into her big, beautiful eyes like I was hypnotized and said, "You!" I couldn't help saying it, she was that pretty. She replied with a smile, "You're silly, besides that, what kind of cookie do you want?"

I didn't even want a cookie. This girl was beautiful, I had to have her number. "Just give me a regular chocolate chip cookie or something!" Then I asked, "What's your name?" She said, "Drea." I replied, "Hello Drea, my name is James." Then I asked her, "Do you have a boyfriend?" She replied, "Yes!" My heart melted. "I kind of figured that, but I had to ask anyway."

I handed her the money and she gave me my change. As I turned to walk away, she said, "But he's not here, though, he lives out of state!" I stopped, turned around jubilantly, and said, "I work over at Buster Browns!" and pointed at the store. "Can I take you out to lunch sometime?" She said, "Sure why not!" Still smiling, she then wrote her number down on my receipt. I took the receipt and said, "I'm going to call you." "I'll be waiting," she replied. I turned and walked away.

I couldn't believe I had gotten her number. I knew there was something distinctive about her and that she was too good for me, but I was determined to see where this would go.

After that experience I walked around the mall killing time, thinking about Drea and how I was going to make her mine. I went back to work and sold more shoes with more confidence than ever before. It's crazy how in life you can meet a person and after a few minutes that person's energy connects with yours and you can actually feel the power, that's how Drea had me feeling.

At that time my life was a trip, I was still trying to find myself and my purpose in life. Things always changed in the blink of an eye. I don't believe in luck, I believe in timing and being in the right place at the right time. That's how I looked at life. We certainly don't have any control over it, you have to go with the flow, every day is a new beginning.

My life was changing quickly. I was doing remarkably good by staying off drugs and not getting into trouble, but in the back of my mind, I would wonder if or when I was going to self-destruct because I had always been my own worst enemy.

We closed the store and I hurriedly walked back around to the cookie store, hoping to get another look at Drea. That's how pretty she was, she had me going crazy, but when I got there she was already gone. I would have to wait to see her another day. As I rode the bus home, all I could think about was her. I had never met such a beautiful, classy black woman in my life before, especially coming from where I had come from. Drea undoubtedly had me going and I hadn't even taken her out, called, or even kissed her yet.

When I arrived home it was late, I was debating if should I call her or not. I decided that I would wait because I didn't want to make it seem as if I were desperate. I took a shower, got into the bed and I would think about her for the rest of the night until I fell asleep.

Game day: It was a beautiful, sunny Saturday afternoon; we were preparing to play our first game. I knew, more than likely, that I wouldn't play, but I would be ready just in case I was called upon. Bruce, Neil and me had lockers right next to each other. As we were getting ready, I looked over at both of them and said, "Even if I don't get a chance to play today, I want to thank you guys for believing in me and pushing me this far. I wouldn't be here if it weren't for y'all!" Neil said, "Man you came a long way. We just planted the seed and you stuck with it, we're proud of you!"

We finished putting on our uniforms and Coach Babcock called us over for that last prep talk. He said, "Guys you've been working hard, now it's time to see if it has paid off. Everyone knows their job, so there should be no reason why we can't go out there and kick their butts,

145

let's get a team prayer!" Then one of the players said a short prayer and we hit the field.

To my surprise the stadium was packed, there were people everywhere. Although West L.A. was a junior college, seeing all of the student body there to support us was a good feeling. All of my life, I was always a dreamer and, even though things didn't work out for me in the Navy, I kept on dreaming. Maybe the Navy wasn't for me, maybe God had another plan. Being on the football field that day, even though it was more than likely I was not going to play, I realized that I could do anything I wanted, as long as I put my mind and heart to it.

The referee blew the whistle for the captains to walk out for the coin toss. Of course, Stephen Baker and the quarterback, Herald Taylor strolled to the middle of the field. We won the toss and the game was on.

They kicked off the ball, we returned it to our 30-yard line and, on the first play, Stephen Baker was split wide left. The quarterback started yelling signals, "Down, set hut, hut!" Baker came off the line, gave the defensive back a quick shake, and just like that, he was sprinting down the field with the defender chasing behind him, but it was too late, the ball was already spiraling into the air.

The pass was perfect. Baker stretched out his arms and the ball dropped right into his hands. As he raced 70 yards to the end zone to score the first touchdown, we all were jumping, screaming and giving high fives to each other as the referee threw up the touchdown sign. At that point I saw why they called Stephen Baker "The Touchdown Maker," he was the man at West L.A.

We won the game that day, 35 to 14. I played in the fourth quarter with five minutes left. Although I didn't get any passes thrown my way, it felt real good actually being on the football field again. Now I had to be patient, keep working hard and my time would come.

I had to work after the game, I couldn't wait to get there to see if Drea would be working that day at the cookie store. When I arrived at Buster Browns to begin my shift, I looked over at her store, but I didn't see her, so I figured she must be off that day, "I'll just call her tonight, I said to myself."

As customers begin to come in, I started selling shoes. It was back-to-school time, so we were really busy. After about two hours it finally slowed down and I started walking around the store, straightening out the display of shoes. The customer bell rang; I turned around thinking it was another sale, it was Drea.

She caught me totally by surprise. "I thought you were going to call me last night," she said. "I got in kind of late, so I didn't want to wake you!" I replied. "That was sweet of you. I just got here, I have to close tonight, so don't forget to come and get your cookie!" I said, "Cool, I'll be over there when I take my break!" "Ok I'll be waiting!" she replied. She blew me a kiss then turned and walked away real slow and sexy.

That was my first time seeing her from behind the counter. Her body was banging hot that ass was nice and tight. I watched as she walked out and was fascinated; Mr. Lee shook his head yes, and gave me the thumbs up. As I continued working, all I could think about was taking my break so I could go get my cookie.

More customers walked in and, after selling a couple of more pairs of shoes, I walked to the front of the store to look out into the mall, I could see the cookie store from there. When I looked out, she was looking down my way as well, she quickly pulled her head back into the store. We had both caught each other taking a sneak peek. I was flattered; my confidence grew. I felt that I just might have a good chance with her after all.

Another hour went by, Mr. Lee said, "James, you take a break, okay?" I said, "Yes sir!," signed out and headed straight to the cookie store. Drea had her back turned counting some money. Nobody was in line. I quietly crept to the counter and said, "Boo!" She turned around quickly. When she saw that it was me, she smiled in relief and said," You scared me!" I just laughed. "Let me finish counting this money, I'll be right there."

There was something extraordinarily different about her, I couldn't quite pinpoint it. She was unlike any other girl I had ever met at the time. I knew that she was too good for me, but I still had to have her. She finished counting the money and walked towards me and said, "So what's up baby?" I was shocked that she had called me baby, the way she said it sounded as if I were actually her baby. I stood there staring at her. She said, "Why are you looking at me like that?" "You are so pretty, where are you from?" "I live in LaDera Heights, but I go to school in New Hampshire."

LaDera Heights is like the black Beverly Hills, but on the opposite side of town, all the rich black folks lived there. As soon as she said that I knew she was out of my league because I lived in the projects, and that was a huge class difference. What she would say next blew me away, "I go to Dartmouth University, have you ever heard of it?" I said, "Isn't that one of those   Ivy league schools?"

149

"Yes, it sure is.. She replied. I honestly just took a good guess when I said Ivy league; Dartmouth just sounded like Harvard or Yale, one of those prestigious colleges.

Then she asked, "What school do you go to?" I proudly said, "West L.A. Junior College!" She had this confused look on her face and said, "Where is that?" I replied, "It's not too far from here. I play football there, we won our first game today!" When I said that, her eyes lit up then she said, "I love football. It's too bad I work on Saturday, it would have been nice to come to one of your games!" I was glad that she worked on Saturday too, because I don't think I could have handled her coming to my game and seeing me ride the bench. I just played it off and said, "Well maybe you could come down to one of my practices sometime." "That sounds like fun, just let me know when!" she replied, as customers begin to line up.

That was my queue to leave. I said, "I'm going to get back to work. I promise I'll call you tonight." She said, "You better!" and blew me a kiss. All I could do was stare and get another good look her again before I left. I walked to the food court to get a bite to eat. I couldn't believe that I had met a girl who attended Dartmouth, I knew that there was something distinctive about Drea, I couldn't wait to talk to her tonight and find out more.

150

That day at work went smoothly, I was getting more familiar with the store and my boss was happy with my performance. We closed up and I headed to the bus stop to go home. I was tired, I just wanted to get home, take a shower, relax and talk to Drea over the phone.

When I got home my mother had fried some chicken, I loved her chicken. Even though she was still dipping and dabbling with drugs, she still maintained and ran the house. My mom asked, "Do you want some chicken La-Ray?" I said, "Yes," went to make me a plate and sat down at the table with her.

She asked, "Did you win your game today?" I replied, "Yes, but I didn't play much." "How is your new job going?" she asked. I replied, "It's going good, I met a good-looking girl that works at one of the stores up there!" She then said, "That's good for you. When do you get paid?" I replied, "Next week." "Ok, because I'm going to need some money!" she said. I responded by saying, "I know mom, don't worry, I got you." She said, "I know you're not getting an attitude with me?" "Nope, I'm just tired!" I replied.

My mother always had a way with me. She knew how to get under my skin, but, at the same time, she knew that I would never disrespect her, regardless of what and she was right. I wish we had those shows like "Intervention" back then. When I watch those shows now I can relate to the people and what they're going through. because their situations were similar to mine. Their drug abuse resulted in their losing homes and jobs and getting on welfare, overall things were going badly for them.

I watched and say to myself, "I can feel your pain."

I finished my food, grabbed the phone, went upstairs to my room and called my dream girl. We talked on the phone for hours. She told me about how she was studying to be a doctor, about her dad playing professional football and about how her boyfriend was not treating her right.

That's one thing I respected her for. Although we had just met, she felt comfortable opening up and sharing with me, whereas I was cautious about the things I would say to her, because I was still in the process of cleaning up my life and I still had a long way to go. I was a "mischievous boy and she was a" good girl." I wondered how long I could hide my past from her, or would it even matter just as long as I was trying to change my life?

When we were about to get off of the phone, I said to her, "I have never met a girl like you before, you're so pretty, smart and kind, I'm glad we met!" She replied, "Awe, that's kind of you, I'm glad we met too!" We agreed to take our lunch break at the same time the next day and meet at a Mexican restaurant in the food court, then we hung up the phone.

I laid there in my bed wondering what I was going to do about this girl. How long will we know each other? Am I a summer fling or is she just naive? Whatever it was, I didn't care, I just wanted to be around her. I knew in my heart that she was too good for me and that we would never have a real future together, but no matter what, I was going to try and make our friendship last forever. I then fell asleep.

I went to work the next day as usual, got into my same routine selling shoes and waited to take my break so I could go see Drea. This day would be different, we both had agreed to take our break together and meet at a Mexican restaurant.

When I arrived, I was surprised to see her standing there waiting for me. She said, "Hi, baby!" Then she walked towards me, hugged me real tight, and gave me a little peck on the lips. I was totally blown away when she hugged me, I could feel the curves on her body and she smelled so good, I didn't want to let her go.

I said, "What's up, sexy, you hungry?" She replied, "Yes!" with a smile on her face, then she grabbed my hand, and we went inside the restaurant. Her hands were extremely soft and smooth; we never let go of each other. Finally we had gotten a chance to spend a little quality time together and get better acquainted.

I said, "I've been waiting all day to see you!" She replied, "Me too!" The waiter then brought glasses of water, menus and chips to the table and said, "How are you today?" "We both said, "Ok." He then said, "I'm going to give you two love birds time to order, I'll be right back." We just looked at each other and laughed; we were still holding hands.

She then said, "Gosh, your hands are big and they feel so rough, I love them!" She squeezed them tighter. I didn't know what to say, I just said, "It runs in the family." She then said, "My dad has enormous hands too!" I started to let my guard down, but said to myself, "This girl truly likes me, I might as well go with the flow."

We looked over the menu, then I asked, "What are you going to order?" She said, "I like their Quesadillas, and you?" I replied, "I think I'm going to try the tacos." "Yum, those are good!" she replied. The waiter came back and asked, "Are you ready to order?" We placed our order and went back to looking into each other's eyes. Drea then said, "I'm going to miss you when I go back to school!"

I was so infatuated by her I had forgotten all about that. I asked, "When are you leaving?" She said, "In two more weeks!" I knew that I would have to make my move and get as close to her as possible before she left. "Two weeks? That's around the corner!" I said. "I know," she replied, then she laid her head on my shoulder. If a person didn't know we had just met the other day, they would have thought that we had been together for a while, from the way she was all over me.

Then she asked, "Can I come to your practice tomorrow? I'm off work and I don't have anything else to do." I said, "Yes, that would be nice." She looked up at me with those big pretty eyes and said, "Kiss me!" I was caught off guard, so I kissed her real quick on the lips. She said, "No, a real kiss!" Then she leaned over and stuck her tongue into my mouth, I could feel the wetness of her kiss as our tongues twirled around in each other's mouths. I was in paradise or so it seemed. I felt as if I were sweltering inside, I began to get aroused. When my dick started to get hard, I had to pull away. She said, "Umm, that felt good. I've been waiting to do that for a while!"

155

I said to myself, "This girl is a super freak."I was relieved when the waiter brought out our food because I think I would have had an orgasm right there on the spot if we kept on loving on each other. "Here you two love birds go." at the same time he put our food on our table. Then said, "Is there anything else that I can get you?" We said, "No thank you," and he left.

I said to her, "You're going to make me fall in love if you keep on kissing me like that!" She then took her hand, put it under the table, and started rubbing my dick. I was shocked and said, "Girl, you better control yourself, we're inside a restaurant!" She said, "Nobody can see!" She started laughing and then we started eating our food.

"So, what time do you want me to come visit you tomorrow?" She asked. I replied, "About four o'clock would be fine." She then said, "Ok, I'll be there baby!" I swear every time she called me baby it made me feel significant, I was certainly becoming her baby. I gave her the directions to West L.A. Junior College. After we finished our lunch, I walked her back to the cookie store. We tongue kissed again. I went back to work with a smile, and lipstick, all over my face.

The next day we had a tough practice. It was hot, and Coach Babcock ran the shit out of us then told us to take a

15-minute break. We were exhausted, guys were laid out all over the field.

I was laying on one of the blocking bags when looked up to see Drea walking towards the practice field, with her long black hair blowing in the wind. As she got closer, I could see that she had on her regular clothes, looking absolutely stunning.

I could hear the guys whispering, saying, "Damn, man, who the fuck is that? She's finer than a motherfucker. "She stopped at the gate and waited; I didn't say anything to the guys, I just got up and started walking towards her. I could hear some of the guys saying, "Soil, sit your ass down, nigga, she's not coming to see you, she must be one of the cheerleaders!" In my mind I was like, "Watch this."

I walked up to her, smiling, she was also. I said, "Hey, what's up, I see you found it, huh?" She said, "Yes," then leaned over and stuck her tongue into my mouth, we started kissing on the spot. My teammates started screaming, and going crazy and shit, yelling my name, saying, "Soil, Soil, Soil!" We pulled away and I said, "Don't mind them, they're silly!"

I grabbed her hand, and we walked over to sit in the bleachers to talk. "So this is West L.A.," she said. "Yup, this is it!" I replied. "Man, you're going to have to stop doing that, I told you you're going to make me fall in love with you!" "Why? You don't like it when I kiss you?" she asked. I said, "Yeah I love it!" "Well what are you complaining about then?" she said. We started kissing again.

All of a sudden the whistle blew. Break time was over and it was time to go back to practice. Drea said, "I'm going to sit here and watch you ok, baby?" I said, "That's cool, baby" and ran back onto the field. When I got back, all of the guys were saying shit like, "Man, I don't know where you met her, but she is gorgeous!" Then I said, real proud, "Yeah, she sure is and she goes to Dartmouth!" They said, "Yeah right, nigga." I just smiled and went to my position coach.

I had a good practice that day, it felt good knowing that Drea was up there watching me practice. Every day we were growing closer and closer. She stayed the entire practice until I was done. We finished practice, I went back over to her, all sweaty. She said, "You looked good out there!" wiping the sweat from my face with her hand at the same time. "God, look how sweaty you are, I just want to feel you all over my body." I said, "You're crazy girl." We kissed again.

There was one thing that I was starting to notice about Drea—she was quite outspoken and not afraid to express her feelings about me. It seemed as though she didn't have anything to hide, I loved that about her. She was a unique individual, I unquestionably liked her.

I said, "Come on, let me walk you to your car so I can take a shower and get my ass to work." I walked her to her car, we kissed some more, this time I got a little bolder and grabbed a handful of her ass. It was round and tight; it felt like a soccer ball. She ground her hips against mine and let out a soft moan; my dick immediately grew hard as our tongues went deeper down each other's throats. I always had to be the first one to pull away whenever we would kiss because, if I didn't, she would just keep going. It didn't matter where we were, she was never afraid to show her passion for me in public.

I knew it would only be a matter of time before we would have sex. Although we had only known each other for a short period of time, we both had that urge. Drea would be leaving soon and time was not our friend. She got into her car, rolled the window down and said, "You got me all wet down there!" I replied, "You got me all hard and horny too, baby." We kissed again, she said, "Call me when you get home, I don't care how late it is!" I said, "Ok, I will, baby!" Then she drove off into the sunset.

I went inside the locker room and had to go through all the hoopla—pats on the back, guys asking me does she have any girlfriends and all that bullshit. I showered, got dressed, and, as we headed to the bus stop, Bruce said, "Damn! James, who was that girl you were kissing all up on at practice?" I said, "She was sexy, huh? You know I got a new job at the mall, right? Well I met her at Mrs. Fields Cookies, she works there!"

Neil said, "You came up man!" I replied, "I know and she really does go to Dartmouth, she's studying to be a doctor. The bad part about it is that she is leaving to go back to school in two more weeks." Bruce said, "You have to hit that before she leaves, dog!" I said, "Man, you know I'm sure going to try." We hopped on the bus.

As we rode home, for some reason I started daydreaming about my mother and how she would tell me stories, when I was younger, about her, my aunt Louise, and my four uncles. They were born and raised in Hope, Arkansas, that's where they actually grew up. Her maiden name was Yerger. She would tell me about Yerger Middle School and a street named after my Great Grandfather, and how my Uncle Sony made a bike out of wood. My mother also told me how she and my uncle Leroy were picking plums one day and he had her fooled her to climb up the tree to pick out this real ripe one, only to get stung by a bunch of wasps that had their nest nearby. She said my uncle just laughed—I didn't find it funny though.

When my mother told me stories about her youth, I would imagine how it must have been growing up in the country. Those were her childhood days; then they moved to Santa Monica. She told me how she met my dad, how tall he was, and how she used to play hard to get, but she had finally given into him because he looked good and would be dressed so elegantly. I guess, when they moved to the big city, they got turned on by the fast pace, and turned out by the drugs.

Reality snapped back in when the business stopped at the mall I had to go to work. I told Bruce and Neil that I would see them tomorrow, we shook hands, then I exited the   bus.

CHAPTER 10

Special Lady

It was a busy night at Buster Browns that evening. I liked it when we were busy because it made the time fly by faster. I only worked for four hours so I was okay. Although I knew Drea wasn't working today, I couldn't stop myself from looking down at the cookie store and thinking about her.

Ten o'clock came and it was time for me to go. I vacuumed the floor, put all the shoes back in place and said, "Goodnight, Mr. Lee, see you tomorrow." He was in the back-counting money. He came out, made sure everything was clean and said, "No, you off tomorrow, James. So far you do a good job, I like you!" I replied, "Thank you, sir!" and ran to catch the last bus.

When I arrived home, my mother was waiting downstairs for me with an envelope in her hand. I said, "Hey, mom, what's up?" She said, "You got some mail from that school you go to, it looks like a check." She handed me the envelope and I opened it up. Sure enough, it was the other half of my PellGrant, $700.

I was surprised, I said to my mother, "It's the other half of my grant money to finish paying for my books and stuff!" I was excited, my mom was happy as well, or should I say impressed, because all this time she had felt that I was wasting my time by going back to school, that I wasn't going to stick with it and it was just a pipe dream. She said, "Go on, boy, do your thing, I'm truly proud of you!" I couldn't believe that she was actually proud of me once again, I could feel it.

I said, "I'm going to give you some money, momma, and finish paying for my books!" She hugged me, then she said something that I needed to hear. She said, "Follow your dreams, son. You can do whatever you want, if you put your mind to it!" I replied, "I will mom, thanks. I needed to hear that from you!"

I grabbed the phone and ran upstairs to call Drea. I dialed her phone, and she picked up on the first ring. "Hello." She said, "Hi, baby, I've been sitting here waiting for your call, what's up?" "Nothing much, I was just talking with my mom," I replied. "Awe, you must be a mama's boy?" I said, "Yep, I sure am. I love her to death!" Drea then said, "That's sweet. I had a pleasant time watching you at practice today, when I left, my pussy was dripping wet!" "You're so naughty, but in a good way!" I replied. She then said, "Well it's the truth, I was really wet down there!" I then said, "You look so pretty and innocent, it turns me on when you talk dirty to me!" "You like it when I talk dirty to you? She asked. "Yes, I love it!" I said.

At that point, I knew I was going to get that pussy. I had received my Pell grant money and decided that I was going to get my sister to rent me a car. I would take her out to dinner and make my move, after all she was leaving in less than two weeks, I had to experience some of her good loving before she left.

I said to her, "You have to let me take you out to dinner before you leave." She replied, "I thought you would never ask, where are you taking me?" I replied, "To this restaurant in the Marina Del Rey called The Warehouse." "Is that where you take all of your girls?" She asked. I then said, "Oh no, you have to deserve it for me to take you there." She then asked, "So I deserve it?" My answer to her question was,"Yes, you do that and more, baby!"

We agreed to go to dinner the next Sunday because that would be her last day working at the mall. We talked for about two more hours, then we got off the phone.

Drea had become more of a motivation to me, I had said to myself, "If you can get a girl like her, you could get any woman of her caliber." Although I wasn't the most handsome guy, I guess there was something about me that attracted her. As I lay down, my mind started playing tricks on me, I had gotten that money, and thoughts of getting high started running through my mind—I immediately blocked them out and went to sleep.

That week went by fast; we had won our second game. I played about the same amount of time I had played the week before, but I wasn't upset though, I was a team player and as long as we won, I was happy. Besides, work was going good, I had some money in my pocket, I was drug free, and I had the prettiest girl I have ever met in my life. I guess you could say I was truly blessed.

That Sunday I went over my sister Tonnetta's house to get her to rent me a car, she had just gotten out of church. I knocked on her door, she opened it and said, "Hey, boy, what's up? You missed a good service today, I prayed for you!" I said, "Thanks!" Then I asked, "Toni, can you rent me a car, so I can take out this girl I met?"

She said, "Boy, you know I don't have money to rent a car!" I replied, "I have the money, you just have to give them your credit card." Tonnetta then said, "Oh, if that's the case, it should be no problem. Let me get out of these church clothes and we can go!" She changed clothes and we went to the rental car company.

When we arrived, we looked over the cars and she asked, "Which one do you want?" I saw a white convertible Camaro, I pointed to it and said, "That one!" She said, "Boy, that cost $49 a day!" I reached into my pocket and gave her $120.00 for the car and $25.00 to put into her pocket for renting it for me. "Where did you get all that money?" "From West L.A. They gave me a grant for my books and stuff, I've also been saving my money from my job!" She said, "I'm quite proud of you, I remember when you got out of jail, everybody said that you would be smoking in a week, but you stayed strong and proved them wrong!"

That's one thing about drugs,when a person gets off of them, some people think it's just a matter of time before they relapse, which a lot of people do, that's why when I had stopped smoking cocaine, I never went around on my soap box professing that I had quit. I just took it one day at a time, and when people would offer them to me, I would say, "No, thanks, and quickly got away from them!

My sister went into the office and did all the transactions, she and the worker came out to inspect the car, she signed the paperwork, he handed her the keys, she jumped in the car and drove it off the lot.

I followed her back to her house with a smile on my face because I was going to kick it later on that night. When we arrived back at her house, she said, "That car is fast, you better be careful. I had to put it under my insurance." I said, "I will, thanks!" I kissed her, jumped in the car, let the top down and was gone. It felt good rolling down the street in that all white convertible. I had the music blasting, and on the radio the song called "C-o-o-l" was playing by the group "Morris Day and The Time. "I headed home to change clothes and to get ready for my date with Drea.

At that time, the television series "Miami Vice" was out, we wouldn't leave the house until that show went off. Crockett and Tubes had niggas in Los Angeles wearing sport jackets, bright ass pastel colors, and slip-on loafers with no socks on—and I was one of them. I arrived home, took a shower and put on my white cotton pants, a blue shirt with yellow, red and green triangular patterns, my white slip-on loafers and a white jacket. Back then I was cleaner than a motherfucker, but now I would have been looking like a damn fool.

I called Drea to get her address, the phone rang about four times. Ring, ring, ring, ring. I had gotten a little nervous, then she picked up. "Hello," her soft and sexy voice said. I said, "What's up, baby, what took you so long to pick up the phone?" "Hi, sweetheart, I'm sorry I was upstairs finishing my hair!" I responded, "I'm about to head your way, what's the address?" She said, "Oh good, it's 2039 Prairie View Rd. Just exit the freeway on La Cienega Blvd and make a left on Prairie View."

I replied, "Cool, I should be there in about 30 minutes!" She said, "Ok, baby, I'll be ready. I can't wait to see you and my mother wants to meet you, bye!" and she hung up the phone. I said to myself, Damn! Her mom wants to meet me, oh shit, now the real test will come.

I hung up the phone, sprayed some Holston's Z-13 cologne on, and knocked on my mother's door to ask how I was looking. Knock, knock! My mother opened her door, I said, "How do I look?" She came out of her room and said, "Go on then, boy, with your bad self, you got that Miami Vice outfit on and you're looking good, La Ray!" She was just smiling away. I said, "This is nothing, come look at this," I grabbed her hand, we went downstairs, and I showed her the white convertible I just rented. She put her hand over her mouth, then pulled it away and said, "Boy, you done went and bought you a new car, too!" I laughed and said, "Naw, Momma, Tonnetta rented it for me."

Then she said, "That girl must certainly be special. Y'all be careful, have an enjoyable time and thank you for the money." Earlier that day, I had given her my whole check from working at my new job to get food and to help with some of the bills. She hugged me, gave me a kiss and I went out the door.

As I was rolling down the street, jamming to the music, it seemed as if I were in another world. Things had finally turned for the better, this is how I wanted it to be. This was the real me, not that crack smoking monster that I had been in the past. I just looked up at the sky and said, "Thank you, God!" as I cruised down the streets of Los Angeles.

I had to make one more stop to pick up some red roses at the store. After picking up the roses, I was on my way to Drea's house. I exited La Cienega Blvd, made a left, went down to Prairie View, made another left and just like that, I was in a whole different side of town, the houses were immaculate.

I had driven through LaDera Heights many times before, but I never had a reason to stop because I didn't know anyone who actually lived in that part of town, now here I was going to pick up my date. As I got closer to the address Drea had given me, the houses got bigger until I ended up at the biggest house on the block at the top of the hill. I had to double check to make sure I was at the right one.

I looked at the address I had written down on paper, and it was. I hesitated for a while, admiring this fat ass house that she lived in. The landscaping looked as if it were something out of Home and Garden Magazine. The house was two stories with a four-car garage, and they had to have at least six bedrooms in that place.

I slowly made my way to the door, down the winding walkway, my heart was beating real fast as I rung the doorbell. The porch light came on and her father answered the door. Man, I swear that dude had to be at least six-foot-five-inches because, when the door opened, all I could see was his stomach. I slowly looked up at him; he was staring down at me. Drea had told me that he had played professional football back in the day, but, hell, that nigga looked as if he still could play.

I reached out my hand and said, "Hi, how are you doing, sir? My name is James." He smiled, stuck out his hand, and said, "How are you doing, young man? My name is Mr. Hayes, come in and have a seat." Drea was not lying—his hands were huge. I went into the house and took a seat. He called for Drea, "Drea, James is here!" She said, "Ok! ``I'll be right down."

Inside of her house was scenic; I had never been inside of a house like that before. They had this grandiose winding staircase, antique pictures all over the walls and the furniture looked real expensive. I was afraid to sit down on it until he requested.

Mr. Hayes said, "I've been hearing a lot of good things about you, James. So you play football, huh?" I replied, "Yes, sir, I'm going to West L.A. Junior College now and I hope to transfer to a university next year!" "You can do it, just stay focused, son. I used to play football. I went to UCLA and then played for the Baltimore Colts until I blew my knee out. Just keep your nose clean, work out and study hard, you will be alright." When he said, "Keep your nose clean," I didn't know if he were talking about snorting cocaine or if it were a figure of speech, but, whatever it was, he had certainly gotten my attention!

Then Drea and her mother came downstairs. She looked immaculate, her hair was long, black and silky, it came down over her shoulders, and it was real, back then weaves were not as popular yet. She said, "Hi, James, what are you two talking about?" As she and her mother walked down the spiraling staircase, she had on an elegant looking dress that was not too long and not too short. I could see her muscular shaped thighs and calves as she made her way down the stairway, they looked as if she were a track star.

I said, "Hello, your dad was down here giving me some good advice!" Then her mom said, "Hey, James, I'm Mrs. Hayes, it's lovely to meet you!" To my surprise, she hugged me and gave me a peck on the cheek. I said, "It's a pleasure to meet you as well, ma'am!" I said "Mam" to let her know that I had respect for her. She then said, "You're so polite and respectful, you don't have to call me ma'am." We made small talk for about ten minutes, then Mr. Hayes said, "Well, we don't want to hold you two up, you guys have a good time tonight!" We shook hands, Drea kissed her father and hugged her mother, and we were out the door.

On the way to the car, I told her how charming her parents were, "Your parents seem to be real chill, I see where you got your personality from." She replied, "Awe, thanks sweetie. They are very friendly, I love them. I could tell that they liked you too." I said, "I was hoping that I would make a good impression!" I open her door, "This is a neat car!" "It's just something I rented for a couple of days." "Oh, you didn't have to do that, I could have picked you up!" she said. I replied, "You probably would've, but I couldn't let you do that on our first date!" I gave her the roses I bought from the store. She smelled them, smiled, and said, "Thank you, baby, I love roses!" She gave me a kiss and we drove off.

"Your parents have a beautiful house, it's humongous, I have never been in a house like that before!" She looked at me kind of dumbfounded and said, "Yes, it's really nice I'll have to show you around before I leave." Then she said something that I wasn't prepared for, she asked, "Where do you live?"

I paused for a minute, then said, "I live in the projects in Culver City." She then looked at me and said, "Are they bad?" but she said it as if she was more fascinated. I said, "Yeah, it can get pretty rough over there sometimes!" Then she said something that was kind of funny, but sweet. "Do you have a gun? My dad has one, two as a matter of fact, I saw them before!" I laughed and said, "Naw, I don't have a gun, but my homeboys do!"

She then said something that would just take me by surprise, "I want to go there and see them, I've never been to the projects before!" I said to Drea, "You don't want to go there, it's not a place for a girl like you." She responded, "You and your boys will take care of me, won't you?" I said to myself, "This girl is so naïve, but in a cool way, and I love it." I replied, "One day when we have time, I'll take you over there." "You promise?" she asked "Yeah, I promise." I said. She then said, "I can't wait!" We exited the highway and pulled into the parking lot of the Warehouse Restaurant.

The valet opened the car doors and said, "Welcome to the Warehouse!" We got out of the car and walked towards the restaurant. The thing that I liked most about the Warehouse was that it had a pond filled with gigantic Goldfish that we could see as we walked over the bridge to enter the lobby. Drea said, "Wow look at those goldfish, they're so big!" I knew she would say something about them.

We entered the restaurant and the hostess greeted us and said, "Welcome to the Warehouse, would you like to dine inside or on the balcony?" I replied, "The balcony is fine." "Ok, follow me!" as we followed her to the balcony, we admired the interior of the restaurant. It had a Hawaiian theme to it, palm leaves everywhere, bamboo torches, and the booths were like miniature huts. She seated us and said, "A waitress will be with you shortly, enjoy your meal." Then she walked away.

Sitting on the balcony gave us a perfect view of the boats docked in the Marina, the Sun was at the end of its descent. As we watched it disappear into the Pacific Ocean, Drea said, "This is so nice and romantic, I'm glad you brought me here!" I said, "I'm glad you came, my friend told me about it, he said it was a pleasant place to bring someone exceptional!"

The waitress then came with menus and water and said, "Good evening, my name is Terry, welcome to the Warehouse. Will you be having any cocktails?" I said, "I'll have a strawberry margarita." Drea said, "Umm, that sounds good, I'll have one as well!" The waitress replied, "Two strawberry margaritas, I'll give you time to go over the menu, be back with your drinks in a minute!" We looked over the menu, I decided on steak and lobster, Drea chose the lemon salmon.

The waitress returned with our drinks and asked if we were ready to order, I said, "Yes" and told her our order. After she took our order and left, Drea was looking across the table into my eyes and said, "Your too far away, come and sit next to me so I can touch you!" I immediately got up and sat next to her, she grabbed my hand and said, "I'm going to miss you so much when I leave!" We just started tongue kissing right there. I pulled away and said, "I'm gonna miss you too, baby." We just sat there holding each other, finishing our drinks and looking out to the ocean.

The waitress arrived with our food. We ate, talked, and enjoyed each other's company. After a while, the waitress came back and asked, "Is everything alright? Can I get you anything else?" I said, "It was delicious, you can bring me the check, thank you!" She brought me the check, I gave her money, and told her to keep the change. She thanked us and we left the restaurant.

Drea said, "Thank you for taking me out to dinner!" I replied, "You don't have to thank me, baby." I gave the valet my ticket and he brought us the car. I said, "What do you want to do now?" She replied with, "Whatever you want to do." She moved over and started kissing me again, this time she reached down and started rubbing my dick.

"We can do anything you want, baby, I'm all yours tonight!"

Unless I was stupid, that was my queue that it was time to get the pussy, but I had to make sure. I said, "What do you mean by that?" She said, "I'm all yours baby, just drive. I don't care where we go or what we do, as long as we're together!" She was kissing me all over, sticking her tongue in my ear and licking my neck. She was hot, horny and ready to fuck!

I put the car in drive and drove off. I knew exactly where I was going to take her, back then it was a hotel in L.A. called "The Snooty Fox"—that's where we would go if we needed to get a nice room to kick it in. It had all the amenities, Jacuzzis in each room, mirrors on the ceiling, color televisions, and they weren't that expensive.

I jumped on the 405 Freeway heading to The Snooty Fox to get a room. As I was driving, she was still all over me, rubbing on me, kissing, and moaning. I got a little bolder and pulled her dress back, slid her panties to the side and started playing with her pussy, it was dripping wet. I couldn't believe how wet it was, it was so wet that when I pulled my fingers out, I could see her cum all over my fingertips. She quickly put my hand back down there and said, "Don't stop, baby!" She was breathing real hard.

I said to myself, damn, she's a freak! I just started finger fucking her faster and faster as she moaned and came all over my hand.

I exited the freeway and sped to the Snooty Fox. I pulled into the parking lot of the hotel, cut the engine off and said, "I'm going to get us a room, okay?" She fell back on the seat and said, "Ok baby, hurry!" she was still breathing hard. I exited the car, and said to myself, "I'm getting ready to fuck the shit out of her." I went inside to pay   for   a   room.

CHAPTER 11

Balling

When I rung the bell, the guy came out from the back room and said, "Can I help you, sir?" I said, "Yes, I need a room for four hours." He said, "Ok, that will be $75, plus tax, all together $84.98." I slid the money to him and he skidded me a white card and said, "Fill this out for me, do you want smoking or not?" I replied, "None smoking." I finished filling out the card, slid it back to him and he gave me the key. I went back to the car to get Drea, I opened the door and asked, "You sure you want to do this, baby?" She nodded, yes, got out of the car and we walked towards the room.

When I opened the door to the room, the Jacuzzi was already bubbling with the red light reflecting from the bottom of it. I turned the clock radio on to KJLH, they were bumping some slow jams. I took off my jacket threw it on the chair, turned to Drea, and we started kissing. As I was rubbing on her tight ass, she wrapped her arms around my neck, and we fell onto the bed. I got on top of her and we started grinding and kissing each other. We kicked off our shoes, then tore off each other's clothes.

I was looking at her body while I was kissing her, she had the most perfect body, not a stretch mark, dent or scar anywhere to be found. Her breasts pointed out like snow cones cups, her nipples just stood up and came to a perfect point.

I put them in my mouth, sucked, and licked them as if I were a little baby. She moaned with ecstasy as she grabbed my penis and slowly began to stroke it up and down. She then rolled over on top of me and started to lick my neck, working her way down to my chest and nipples, we were both breathing hard and heavy. I could feel her passion, she kept going further down to my navel. I thought she would stop there, but she kept going, then she did something that I wasn't expecting.

She spit on my dick, started licking it up and down, then she put it in her mouth and began to perform oral sex on me. I let out a slight moan and just gave into her control. I couldn't believe what was happening to me, it felt so good. I opened my eyes and just watched in amazement as her pretty face bobbed up and down with my penis in her mouth. She came back up, looked me in my eyes and said, "I want you to fuck me!"

She laid on her back and I climbed on top of her; she spread her legs wide open and I put my dick inside of her. It felt as if it were a hot knife slicing through butter, her pussy was warm, tight and wet. She let out a loud scream and wrapped her long legs around my back. She then wrapped her arms around my neck and started moving like a fish out of water, our bodies moved in unison as we made sweet love.

Sweat was running down my face, she wiped it off with her hand and said, "Oh baby, it's so good, don't cum yet, please don't cum!" I'm not going to lie, I was right on the verge of having an orgasm, but I slowed down, kept my rhythm and held on.

We made love for about thirty minutes, then she said, "It's so wet down there I can feel it, I'm getting ready to cum!" I started fucking her harder and faster, then she screamed, "I'm C-U-M-M-I-N-G!" her legs started trembling, she hugged me real tight and started biting me on the neck. Then I came, we both had an orgasm at the same time.

I held her tight as my sperm squirted inside her pussy. I didn't care if she got pregnant or not, that's how good the pussy was—luckily, she didn't though. We just laid there connected to each other from the sweat of our bodies. I finally got the strength to pull away. I rolled off of her, totally exhausted. She looked over at me and said, "God, that was so good, I've never came like that before!"

I just lay there staring at the ceiling. She then said, "Are you alright, baby?" I said, "Yes, I just want you to know that you really mean a lot to me. I know we have only known each other for a short time, but I have the utmost respect for you and you will always be special to me, no matter what!" She said, "Awe, baby, you are so sweet and kind, I feel the same way. Let's get into the Jacuzzi!"

We hopped out of the bed and got into the Jacuzzi. I put some bubble bath in the water and foam started rising. We played around for a while and made love a couple more times. Then we had to leave, it seemed like time had just flown by.

We got dressed and left The Snooty Fox. I pulled in front of her house, we talked for a while then kissed goodnight. I went home feeling as if I were on top of the world. The next day we went horseback riding at a ranch in Valencia, CA after that, sadly enough, was my last time that I would ever see her again. Drea had to go back to

New Hampshire earlier than planned because her internship at a hospital had opened. She had to report there ASAP, or would have to wait another six months for an opening.

I guess I was just a summer fling, but she did leave me with one thing—courage. From then on, I made it a point that any girl I ever met after that would be like Drea or better, and I would never be ashamed of where I was from, or my class status. I said to myself, " I could get a girl like Drea, I could get any woman that I wanted."

Football season was coming to an end, we had one more game left against Los Angeles Community College, they were 0-9 and we were 6-3. I knew I would play that game, it would be no way possible that I wouldn't, and I was ready.

On the day of the game, in the pre-game speech, Coach Babcock called us together and said, "Gentlemen! This is our last game, I don't want you guys to take this team lightly, go out there and kick their asses and play them like they're 9-0. We're going to get everybody in today, I have a lot of guys leaving this year, and I need to get a good look at the guys who are returning next year, so be ready when I call you." I looked over to Bruce and

Neil, they shook their heads up and down like, "Yeah." We said a prayer and took it to the field.

The game was a total blow out, at half time we were leading 42 to zip, by the early fourth quarter we were leading 56 to 8. Then, all of a sudden, Coach Babcock looked over at me and said, "Soil, are you ready?" I replied, "Yes sir!" He said, "The next play get ready to go in for Walker."

I went and stood next to him so he could give me the play. I could hear the guys in the background saying, "Come on, Soil, this is your chance, let's see you break one, baby!" Coach Babcock grabbed me by my shirt, as he did to Stephen Baker and Bruce Walker, when he told them the play, I always wanted him to do that. He then bent over, whispered in my ear and said, "Slot right wing left, crossbuck reverse on two!" Then he slightly pushed me onto the field.

The play was coming to me and this would be my chance to show everyone what I had. My heart was pounding as I ran towards the huddle yelling, "Walker, Walker out!" Bruce Walker looked up and started running off the field. As we passed each other, we stuck out our hands and gave a high five.

I ran into the huddle and told the quarterback the play, he said, "That's you, Soil!" Then he called the play, "Slot right wing left, crossbuck reverse on two ready!" Everybody said, "Break!" and we broke out of the huddle. I ran to the scrimmage line, got into my two-point stance, and looked at the defensive back right into his eyes.

The quarterback started calling signals, "Ready, set, hut, hut! The center hiked the ball. Suddenly everything slowed down. I took one jab step off of the scrimmage line to make it seem as if I were going to run up the field to let the play develop. I quickly turned and started running towards the backfield. The quarterback pitched the ball to the running back and he started running towards me as if it were a sweep. I then opened my arms and he stuffed the ball into my stomach. I clamped down on the ball and ran wide around the backfield.

I was in full speed when I turned the corner. The defensive end tried to reach out and grab me, but, to my surprise, he missed. The linebacker then came up and I threw him a juke move. All could see was him flying right by me. I heard him say, "Shit!" as he missed. I then saw the back of Stephen Baker in front of me, blocking the last defender and forcing him to the inside, that's all I needed. I went around them and all I could see was green grass in front of me, everything sped up as I raced 80 yards down the field to score. I got to the end zone, turned around, and held the ball up in the air as the referee held his arms up signaling "Touchdown"—everybody went crazy. I dropped the ball and the next thing I knew, Big Neil ran onto the field, picked me up and said, "You scored, I'm proud of you, dog, I'm proud of you!" I was elated!

In my opinion, there's no better feeling than scoring a touchdown, hearing the roar of the crowd and having all of your teammates patting you on the back congratulating you. I loved that feeling, it was an emotional high that no drug in the world could compare to it.

Neil put me down and I ran back to the sideline. Coach Babcock and Coach Smith were smiling at me, they both said, "Good job, Soil!" and gave me a high five. I went and took a seat on the bench to catch my breath and the water boy brought me some water. I sat there, replaying in my mind what I had just done, while my teammates continued to congratulate me.

That was a turning point for me. I played the remainder of the game and we won 63 to 14. After the game, Coach Babcock called everybody together for our last pep talk and said how proud he was of us and how he couldn't wait for next year, then he thanked us. We had our last team prayer and then we left the field headed to the locker room to turn in our uniforms.

As Bruce, Neil and me rode the bus back to the projects, we all were basking in my 80 yard touchdown run. Bruce said, "Damn! James, you got your freak on today when you turned that corner. I told everybody he's taking it all the way!" Then Neil said, "Yeah, man, I had just finished getting my ankle wrapped when I heard everybody screaming. I looked up and all I could see was the back of your jersey going into the end zone." "I just got up, ran onto the field and picked your ass up, I couldn't help it!" I replied, "I was just trying to get a first down, but when I got past that first guy, and saw Baker blocking the defensive back, I was like, fuck it, I'm just going to punch it in and score!"

Running a touchdown gave me the confidence I needed. I had made up my mind that day, I was ready to take it to the next level and set my sights on transferring to a university. I didn't care where I went, but I was going to do everything in my power to get there.

That year of going to West Los Angeles Junior College, playing football, and working came and went. Mr. Lee was bought out by another shoe store called "Stride Rite." Stride Rite brought in their own employees, so I had to find another job. This time it was at the local grocery store called "Lucky's," where I was a stock clerk.

My mother's appetite for drugs had begun to diminish. She had a spiritual awakening and became a "born again Christian," this made me so happy. Her friend, Carolyn, and Miss Mildred had finally gotten to her with all those bible studies. She slowly, but surely, stopped smoking cocaine and started attending church on a weekly basis. I had stayed strong with my battle with cocaine as well. I'm not going to lie, when I first stopped smoking it was hard, I would have those thoughts of getting high, but being on probation and going to the drug classes had kept me in line.

One day I was on the bus coming home from work and the bus had come to my stop in front of the projects. As I got up from my seat to exit out of the back door, I saw one of the local drug dealers stashing something under a trash can. Then he ran, jumped into the car with some other guys, and they took off. He didn't see me. I exited the bus and said to myself, "What did that little nigga put under there?"

No one was around when I walked up to the trash can, picked it up and, low and behold, it was a sack filled with crack rocks. I looked around to make sure nobody was watching, then I quickly reached down and grabbed the baggie, put it in my pocket and continued walking home.

As I walked home, my mind was racing profusely. Was I going to try and sell this shit? Relapse? Smoke it or what? My body and soul were immediately at war. My stomach was bubbling with anticipation as I got closer to my house. I didn't have a pipe, andI couldn't let my mother know because she had stopped smoking. I couldn't get her started again; I would just make a pipe out of the television antenna, smoke a little and that would be it.

I got to my front door, put my hand on the doorknob and, all of a sudden, I heard water gushing down from the creek that was right next to my apartment, something told me to walk over there. I walked to the creek where the water was rushing down real fast. I reached into my pocket, pulling out the crack rocks, opened the bag, and dumped the rocks into the creek. I then let the bag go and watched as the rocks hit the water and the bag slowly floated away.

The cravings left and things went back to normal. I said to myself, "Man, all the time I was on drugs I hustled, stole, lied, connived and drugs have never fallen into my hands like that before." Now that I was clean, drugs tried to find a way to creep back into my life. I realized that it was a test, the devil had tried to pull me back in, but my soul was strong, and it would not give into the craving of my body that day.

I walked into the house to see my mom in the kitchen making dinner. She said, "Hi, son, how was your day?" I said, "Ok, I'm starving though!" She said, "The food will be done in a minute." I didn't tell her about the incident, I didn't want to bring it up. We both were doing well, and we didn't need any distractions.

School had started again and Neil had bought an old Chevy, so we didn't have to catch the bus to West L.A. anymore. We checked in, got our classes as we did the year before, and got into the same routine of going to school and then football practice.

One day at practice Coach Babcock said, "Listen up, guys, we're not going to go against the defense today. I'm going to need some of you to play defense in our one-one drills. Do I have any volunteers?" I played wide receiver and defensive back, so I raised my hand along with some other guys. I figured, "What the hell? I need to do anything I can to try and start this year." Besides, this would show the coaches that I was a team player.

The receivers lined up on one side and we were on the other. Bruce Walker stepped up to the scrimmage line first with me on the coverage. The quarterback began to call the signals, "Ready, set, hut!" Bruce took off, I back peddled to keep a cushing between us and waited for him to break. He did a stutter step and broke toward the post.

I was right on him, the quarterback released the ball and, at the last minute, I jumped in front of him and intercepted it. I couldn't believe it was so easy. Bruce looked at me side eyed as if I were supposed to let him catch it. In my mind I said, "I wasn't going to let him make me look amateurish." Coach Babcock said, "Good job, Soil, that's how you do it. I want you to give them a good look, just as if they were a game!"

As more reps went by, my turn came up again. This time it was one of the new young receivers. just out of high school, he was an All-American, but he had to come to West L.A. to bring up his grades. I said to myself there was no way that I was going to let this little young ass nigga catch the ball on me!

He stepped to the line of scrimmage, the quarterback barked off the signal, and he took off up the field. Once again, I patiently stayed in my back pedal until he made his move; he planted his foot and cut across the middle of

191

the field. As soon as he reached out to catch the ball, I hit him hard as I possibly could—the ball went flying and so did he.

I landed on top of him. When I got up, I said, "Welcome to West L.A!" I could see the fear in his eyes, he didn't think I was going to hit him that hard. I wasn't supposed to, but I did anyway because I was pumped up and I was looking for a starting position. To my surprise, Coach Babcock said, "That's how you are going to get hit in the game son, so you better get used to it!"

I was on a roll, but the test would come. A couple of more reps went by and now it was me against Stephen Baker. I knew Baker was quick and fast, if I were going to stop him, I would have to give him a good bump off the scrimmage line. This would knock him off his route, just a little, then I could keep up with him.

The quarterback again started calling signals, "Ready, down, set!" When he said, "Set,"I ran up and got right in Baker's face man-to-man. The quarterback continued, "Hut, hut!" I got a good jam on Baker, he wasn't expecting me to come up to bump him, and he stumbled, then recovered, and took off up the field. That's all I needed.

I was right on his hip as we raced up the field. I kept my eyes on him, as soon as he looked up and reached out his arms, that was my time to turn around and make my move. I turned around, saw the ball floating in the air, and reached out at the last minute. Right when Baker thought he had the ball, I slapped it out of his hands. All I could hear was, "Oh shit!" and "Awe!" from the guys watching.

Coach Babcock was looking at me in amazement and said, "That was perfect coverage, Soil!" Baker was surprised as well, he just stared at me.

I continued to dominate that day on the scout team, I couldn't be stopped. I had made up my mind that it was now or never, I couldn't afford to hold anything back. After we wrapped up the one-on-one with the receivers, it was time for conditioning. Coach Babcock told us to run four laps and take it in.

As we ran around the field, I noticed the coaches were looking at me and talking to each other. They didn't take their eyes off of me. I was saying to myself, "I hope I'm not in trouble or anything." I continued running my laps and took it in when I finished.

The next day at practice we had our team meeting, then we split up into our positions. As usual, I went with the wide receivers. When I got over there Coach Babcock said, "Soil, you're on defense now, report to Coach Smith!" Everybody just looked in bewilderment, I did too. I had performed so well the other day that they switched me to defensive back. Now I knew why they were watching me.

I eagerly ran over to Coach Smith and said, "Coach Babcock told me to come over here!" He replied, "Yep, you're a defensive back now, how do you feel about that?" I said, "It's cool with me, Coach, I just want to contribute to the team anyway I can!" He then said, "That's the right attitude," and he threw me a gold shirt. "Here, put this on!" Coach Smith said.

The defense wore three different shirts, black for the first team, gold for the second team and red for the third team. I was happy to have a gold shirt' I felt that I would have a better chance of playing on defense. Over there they had a guy named Ron Beaks at strong-safety, Jr. Thurmond, the brother of Dennis Thurmond, formerly of the Dallas Cowboys at Free-Safety, Lonny Wilmore at left cornerback and, of course, my boy Bruce Hadley at right cornerback.

We went through all of the defensive drills; I caught on quickly. After we did all the drills, Coach Babcock blew the whistle—it was time for the receivers, defensive backs, linebackers and running backs to go seven-on-seven.

The starting defense went against the second team offense and the first team offense went against the second team defense. On the first play, the All-American freshman took Wilmore deep and caught the ball for a touchdown. Coach Smith just shook his head in discouragement.

On the next play, the youngster beat Wilmore again on a curl pattern. Wilmore went for the interception and missed the ball. The young All-American caught it and turned up the field. I was like damn this guy; Wilmore is not having a good day.

On the following play, the quarterback threw it to the tight end. Beaks came up and knocked the shit out of him and then he dropped it. They blew the whistle.

Now it was time for the second team to go in. I had a repeat performance of the day before, although I didn't get any interceptions. I stopped Baker and Walker from catching the ball on my side; preventing them from catching the ball was not an easy task.

The first defense went in again and the All-American went back to work on Wilmore, beating him on a stop-and-go. When he caught the ball, Coach Smith put his hand on his hips. To everyone's disbelief, Wilmore came running back with a smile on his face. I don't know if he was cocky because he led the team in interceptions the previous year, or what, but Coach Smith was not impressed! As Wilmore ran back to the huddle, Coach Smith yelled, "Wilmore! What the hell is so GODDAMN funny! You think it's a joke out here? Well how about this then?" What he would say next made everybody stop in their tracks!

He then said, "Wilmore, take off your black shirt and give it to Soil!" My eyes opened wide and my heart almost jumped out of my chest. I quickly stood up, took off my gold shirt and tossed it over to Wilmore; he slowly took off his black shirt and threw it to me. I put on my black shirt and said to myself, "I'm never going to take off this black shirt." Then Coach Smith said, "Get out there, Soil!" As all eyes were on me I jogged onto the field. Bruce looked at me, smiled and shook his head, yes!

I had made it to the first team, my hard work and dedication had paid off. I then realized that I could do anything in this world that I wanted to, if I put my mind to it. We continued going seven-on-seven. I don't know if the planets had lined up or the receivers were scared of me, but when I ran my first play on the starting defense, the quarterback threw the ball my way on a quick out. I intercepted it and ran up field. Coach Smith looked at Wilmore and said, "Now that's how you play cornerback!" Wilmore put his head down in defeat.

CHAPTER 12

Triumph

We started off the season with a blast while winning our first six games and losing one. I was leading the team with four interceptions, 52 tackles, and three fumble recoveries. I was also third in leading the league in kick-off-returns.

The next game would determine if we would go to the play-offs or not. It was against Pierce Community College. They were 7-0 and had this wide receiver with the same status as Stephen Baker and Bruce Walker—it was my job to stop him!

He was a tall ass white boy that was about six-feet-two-inches and 190 pounds. I was six feet and 180 pounds. Bruce and I would stay after practice every day and watching film on him. Bruce said, "Damn, James, that's a big mother-fucker!" I replied, "Hell, yeah, I'm just going to have to intimidate him and give him a couple of Atk's to the head!" Atk was a short name for George Atkinson from the Oakland Raiders. He was one of the dirtiest players in NFL and was our idol. Atkinson would elbow guys in the head or necktie a person ferociously when he tackled them. Bruce just laughed.

At practice, a day before the crucial game, Coach Babcock called us together and said, "Ok, guys, this is the game we have been waiting for, winning it will get us into the play-offs. It will be a night game. They have an Astroturf field so I would advise you to wear long sleeve shirts, gloves and a pair of good tennis or turf shoes. That artificial turf will give you rug burns, so you don't want to have any bare skin showing."

He continued, "We've had some good practices, so continue to work hard. Let's take it to them on Saturday. Get a team break and take it in." We all gathered close together and put our hands together. Then Beaks said, "Oilers on three 1, 2, 3." We all yelled, "O-I-L-E-R-S!"

After practice, Bruce said, "Fuck wearing some tennis shoes, let's go to Big-5 and buy some Astroturf shoes!" I said, "Hell, yeah and, since we're wearing our all white uniforms, we might as well get some white Sanitariums, white thermals and some white gloves." "Sanitariums" are some long socks that go past your knees. We showered up, got dressed and went to Big 5

Sporting Goods to get all the necessary gear we needed for Saturday's game.

Game day: We arrived at West L.A. campus at three o'clock, got taped up and ready for the game. Our away uniforms were sweet. The pants were white, double knit with white satin in front, with a thick blue stripe and two thin gold stripes going down the side. The jerseys were white with blue numbers, gold trimming and an oil tower on the side of the sleeve, and the helmets were blue with gold WLA letters on the side.

We put on everything, but our shoulder pads. We had this humongous mirror in the locker room that everybody on the team was in front of it admiring how clean they were. We made sure that we looked good in our uniforms; that day we were all sharp and clean looking.

We boarded the bus and were on our way to Pierce College. Coach Babcock said, "Ok, guys, it's time to start thinking about your job assignments. I don't want to hear a sound on this bus, is that understood?" We all said, "Yes, sir!" and everything went quiet. All we could hear was the sound of the bus engine roaring down the highway!

When we arrived at the stadium, it was jam-packed, standing room only. I had never played on artificial turf before, I stepped onto the AstroTurf field and I could feel the bottom of my shoes gripping to the turf as I took every step—I was glad I'd bought them. I said, I'm going to break one tonight, I could feel it in my bones.

After we did our calisthenics and pre-game drills, we returned to the locker room to put on our shoulder pads and had a last minute prep talk. Everyone finished getting ready and then Coach Babcock called us all together and said, "This is it, gentlemen, you have to go out there and give it all you got. Play your hearts out and don't have any regrets. We need good blocking on the kick-off return, we have some guys back there who can run it back!"

I knew he was talking about me and that pumped me up even more. He continued, saying, "So hold on to your blocks and let's jump on them early. Beaks, let's get a team prayer." Beaks said a short prayer, we put our hands together and said, "Oilers!" and took it to the field.

I loved the adrenaline that I got from playing football. It was a high, but it was a natural high, a person couldn't buy it or smoke it, but rather they had to achieve or earn it, and only when they did something spectacular could they feel it.

After they had sung the "Star Spangled Banner," the referee blew the whistle for the captains to take the field.

Our quarterback, Herald Taylor, and Stephen Baker headed to the center of the field for the toss of the coin. As I watched from the sideline, I was anticipating that we would win the coin toss so I could bust one wide open on the first play, that's just how pumped up I was! The referee threw the coin up, when it hit the ground, he signaled that we won the toss, Baker chose to receive the ball.

I strapped on my chinstrap and jogged onto the field, with poise, ready to do my thing. I had never felt so much self-confidence before; that night I felt I couldn't be stopped. As usual, my heart was pounding. I knew that once I received the ball that everything would slow down. After all, playing football was my new high and I had to get my fix.

The referee blew the whistle, they kicked the ball off, and it went really high. I waited patiently for it to come down; all I could see were bright lights and a brown football spinning in the air—it finally fell into my arms. I quickly dashed up the field, running fast and hard, trusting that my teammates would block for me and open up just a little crease so I could burst through it.

Just as I had wished, a little hole opened up. I squeezed through it and took off down the field. All I could see was green Astro-Turf in front of me and the pink pylons in the corner. I said to myself, "I'm gone!" Just when I thought I was in the clear, I felt a tug on the back of my collar and the defender snatched me to the ground!

I quickly jumped up and started yelling, "HELL YEAH, HELL YEAH! They can't stop us, let's go O!" as the offense ran onto the field. Everybody was pumped up; yelling and patting my back saying, "Good return," and "Way to run the ball, Soil!" I went and stood on the sideline to cheer the offense on. The very next play the quarterback hit Baker with a touchdown pass in the back of the end zone. I swear that guy Stephen Baker was a beast and now I understood why they called him "The Touchdown Maker."It seemed as if he were always guaranteed to score.

We kicked the ball off; it was time for me to go head-to-head with one of the best receivers in the league, a stocky white boy named Ken Noland. My plan was to try to intimidate him and to knock him off his game. When they broke the huddle, he ran to the scrimmage line. I noticed that he was taller and lankier and not as thick as he looked on film. I was going to bump him extremely hard and stay on his hip.

203

The quarterback called the signals, "Ready, set, hut, hut!" I quickly ran up and bumped him real hard when he turned to run up field and then I gave him an "Atk" to the side of the helmet. After the play was over Noland looked at me as if I were crazy, which I was when I was on the football field. Then I said to him, "It's going to be like that all day, bitch, so you better get used to it!" He looked at me and instantly gave me the finger as he ran back to the huddle.

My plan was working. That first series we shut them down, but they were able to kick a field goal. The score was seven to-three, it was a vicious battle as both teams struggled back in fourth to see who was going to make it into the play-offs.

Late in the second quarter Baker and Taylor connected again putting us ahead 14 to-three. Half-time came and both teams left the field.

When we got into the locker room, Coach Babcock said, "Alright, guys, we still have another half to go. Don't get too relaxed, the game isn't over. We have to stay on top of them and keep hammering until the end!" We discussed some offense and defensive schemes, cooled off, and rested before we would take the field again.

When we took the field, Pierce didn't waste any time scoring. On the ensuing kick-off they returned it to our 45-yard line. Noland had caught two short passes on me, but not without paying the price. Whenever he would catch the ball, I made sure that I hit him as hard as I possibly could, slamming him brutally to the ground. I was going to play this way all night until the referee gave me a warning to stop, but he never did, it was the play-offs, so they just let us play.

The next play they did a draw, caught us slipping and ran it straight down the middle of the field to score a touchdown. The score was now 14 to 10 and we had a ball game. As I went back to receive the kick, I was hyped. I knew I had to get another good run to put the offense in good scoring position. The referee blew the whistle and they kicked off again.

This time the ball was high, but short, so I let it bounce and come to me. When the ball bounced, it went kind of high. I jumped up to catch it as I was looking up and reaching out my hands to grab it, I felt the top of a helmet come crashing into my chin. I saw a bright blue flash and, all of a sudden, everything went blank. I had gotten "knocked the fuck out!"

I don't know how many seconds went by, but, when I awoke, all I could see were the trainers, coaches and referees bending over me putting smelling salt under my nose. The trainer put up some fingers and said, "How many fingers do you see?" It seemed as if he had about 20. Everything was blurry and it seemed as if his fingers were going in a circle, and up and down. I said, "I don't know, Coach, they keep moving!" Then the referee said, "He can't go back in, he has a concussion!"

They helped me to my feet. As I got up and walked to the sideline I could hear the applause from the crowd. I said to Coach Babcock, "I can go back in, Coach, I feel better now!" The coach said, "We can't let you go back in, Soil, it's the rule!" They sat me on the bench, then the trainer helped me take off my shoulder pads. I sat on the bench watching helplessly as the white boy, Ken Noland, took total advantage of Wilmore.

We lost the game 27 to 17, and our chance to go to the play-offs. After the game, we went to the middle of the field and shook hands. Ken Noland said to me, "You're not talking all that shit now, bro!" I just looked at him, smiled and gave him the middle finger.

We went on to play the rest of our season for pride, winning our last two games. After the Pierce game, I started receiving letters from small colleges across the country, like Chadron State, University of St. Louise and University of Southern Colorado, just to name a few, but they were not offering me a scholarship. They all wanted me to take out loans and get financial aid. I wanted a full scholarship, so I just held out a little longer, but if I had to go to one of those schools I would have.

Some of the guys had already signed their letters of intent—Steven Baker signed with Fresno State University, Bruce Walker to Prairie View A&M, Ron Beaks to the University of Pittsburgh, Junior Thurmond to University of Southern California, Bruce Hadley to Fort-Hays State, and Neil Windham to New Mexico State. I hope and prayed that some school would give me a full ride, after all, I finished the football season with seven interceptions, five fumble recoveries, over 100 tackles, 22 pass break-ups and was third in the league in kick-off returns!

One day I was coming home from work and when I opened the door, my sister was there cooking. I loved her food. She said, "Hey, boy, it's about time you came home!" She had this odd smile on her face. I said, "What's up, girl, what are you doing over here?" She replied, "To celebrate!" Then she called out to my mother, "Momma, Ray is here!"

I asked, "Celebrate what?" My mom came down the stairs and she was smiling as well. I said, "What are y'all up too?" My mom had her hands behind her back as if she were hiding something. At that moment it reminded me of when I was a little kid and she would come home from work with a surprise for my sister and me. She pulled her hands from around her back, she was holding an envelope.

She said, "This came in the mail for you today. It's thicker than all of the letters you have received, I think this is the one!" I quickly grabbed the letter from her hand. I could feel that it was thicker and heavier than all the letters I had previously got. I looked on the front to see where it had come from, it had Northwest Missouri State University Bearcats, with a giant cat paw on it. I ripped it open and pulled out the contents.

It read: "Dear James Soil, we here at Northwest Missouri State University have been following your football career at West Los Angeles Junior College, and we have decided among the Administration, Sports Director and Football Coaches to award you a full athletic scholarship to play football for the Northwest Missouri State University Bearcats. Enclosed is all the information about our campus, please fill out the Letter of Intent and send it back as soon as possible. Once we have received your Letter of Intent, one of our coaches will call you with further information!"

My heart started pounding. I looked at my mom and started screaming, "I GOT A SCHOLARSHIP! I GOT A SCHOLARSHIP!" She said, "Go on, boy, with your bad self. I'm so proud of you, you did it!" We all started hugging each other and jumping up and down in triumph!

I couldn't believe that I had just been awarded a full athletic scholarship to a university. I had come a long way since getting in trouble, doing drugs, getting dismissed from the military, and everything else that was trying to ruin my life, but I was a dreamer. I always believed that dreams do come true, all you have to do is stick to them and believe in yourself, no matter what anybody else says or thinks. If you set your mind to it, anything is possible.

That following semester I transferred to Northwest Missouri State University, played football for two more years and graduated with a degree in Broadcasting/ Mass Communications. I had a free agent tryout with the Dallas Cowboys, I blew my ankle out and went on to work behind the scenes in Hollywood.

I currently run my own digital record label, S-Line Digital Media Entertainment, and I also work with various hip-hop and R&B artists in Atlanta, Georgia. Although I had won my battle with cocaine, the war on drugs would not be over, the struggle continues.

The End!

Contact Links

Follow on,

- Facebook.com/ James soil
- @smileyvsl Instagram
- gmail: jssoil@gmail.com
- Twitter: @smileyvsl
- Pinterest/ James Soil

9 780578 596525